HOW TO BUILD A WEBSITE FOR FREE!

By Krikor Barsoumian

ISBN – 978-0-557-07402-0

Cover Design: Krikor Barsoumian

Book Design: Krikor Barsoumian

HOW TO BUILD A WEBSITE FOR FREE!

First and foremost, I would like to thank and congratulate you for purchasing this book. You have just purchased the most important instrument in the construction of your website. Thousands of hours of FREE website building techniques, tips and strategies are at your disposal. We will create a beautiful and striking website for little or no money. The step by step website building model is simple, begin with chapter 1 and finish with chapter 21. Every aspect is covered, and search engine optimization results are documented.

How would you like to have a top 10 Yahoo & MSN ranking in less than 3 months. Other companies and individuals spend years attempting to achieving these types of search engine results.

Yahoo	MSN	
# 3	# 14	**Domain Created on:** March 22 2009
# 4	# 9	Domain age (approximately): 2 Months, 15 days.
# 3	# 5	

I emphasize the word FREE in this book repeatedly, to make a point.....website construction does not cost a lot of money, contrary to what many people may want you to believe. All it takes is a basic understanding of computers, the passion to create something significant that will be of benefit to the public or yourself, and time. In the ensuing chapters, we will walk through every aspect of FREE website creation in detail. A few of the FREE website promoting practices that are very easy to implement are:

- Using Free Templates
- Using Free Scripts
- Using Free Images, Pictures & Graphics
- Using Free Software

Anyone can build a successful website for very little cost out of pocket. You do not need to be a millionaire or spend an exorbitant amount of money to achieve the results you are looking for. Using the internet and FREE resources available, we will build a website that looks amazing.

This book is written in plain simple English to educate, assist and motivate the reader in building their dream website. I have eliminated the usual fluff and techno-babble associated with website creation. We will use detailed walkthroughs, graphs and examples to guide you through the entire process.

It is true that many websites out there are very complex and cost thousands of dollars in set up and maintenance. However, for the average person on a budget, this book will show you the FREE route of web building that no one else will dare show you.

TABLE OF CONTENTS - CHAPTERS

TABLE OF CONTENTS - CHAPTERS

FINDING A GOOD NAME

The first and most obvious step in website building and subsequently it's success or failure depends primarily upon selecting a good name. Individuals on the path to building a website (like yourself), have almost certainly already chose a website name. And, there is no right or wrong method for choosing. A website name can take any form, however, we should seriously consider having the same website and domain name.

A website name is the name of your company or website. For example: If your company name is ACME PLUMBING and that is the name you will put at the top of your website, that's your WEBSITE NAME. However, that has nothing to do with the domain name that you may choose.

Website Name vs Domain Name – Not the same thing

The DOMAIN NAME or url is the 'WWW' name and extension of your site -- www.yourwebsite.com. Domain names can be of any length up to 67 characters long. Ideally we should strive to achieve the same website and domain name. In this example, it would be www.acmeplumbing.com.

Choosing a website name is very important from a marketing point of view as well. Imagine if your company (or website) is called "widgets", but somebody else owns that domain name (www.widgets.com). Therefore, you reluctantly chose another domain name for your site like www.otherwidgets.com. What happens when your customers, recalling that widgets co. has a product they want to purchase. They type in www.widgets.com and end up at your competitor's website resulting in a lost sale for you. All this based upon your website and domain name. Something to think about.

Let's also try to implement 'KEYWORDS' (discussed in later chapters) into our website and domain name as well. The most important way your customers will find you is through a search engines caching of your website. Think of it as a snapshot of your website's content. These search engine's look for relevant keywords and use complex algorithms to determine a website's internal structure. An example of a great company name that reflects the nature of the business (selling batteries) and good search engine keywords is www.batteries.com. This is a prime example, of how a good website and domain name can significantly increase the traffic and sales of a company.

When choosing a good domain name let's not over shorten the title. It is true that having a simple, short domain name or url is a good idea, however, let's not lose the clarity of name over the super acronyms that are far too prevalent on today's internet. Instead of choosing a name like www.ERAS.com which is nice and short, it is also very vague and doesn't tell the customer anything about the company. It would be better to call it www.ELECTRONICSREPAIRANDSALES.com.

A good name is crucial when setting up a website. The next step is checking to see if your domain name is available. You may check to see if your domain name is available at any web hosting provider. Anyone can check to see if any domain is available 100% FREE of charges. Check as many domains as you like until you find one that is available. Let's walk through the procedure:

- Once you are connected to the internet, type in "domain name search" in the address bar. (It doesn't matter what internet browser you are using, Explorer, Mozilla, Msn, etc)

- This will bring up a numerous amount of domain name searching links. It does not matter which you log onto. Type in your desired website (domain) name. This will instantaneously let you know if your name is available, and/or what extensions may also be available. Let's use my favorite

"IXWEBHOSTING.COM". Simply plug in the name you would like and they will check to see if it's available.

Along with the domain name there are a variety of extensions to choose from. For example:

www.yourwebsite.com
www.yourwebsite.net
www.yourwebsite.org

- There are many website extensions to choose from:

.com represents the word "commercial," and is the most widely used extension in the world. Most businesses prefer a .com domain name because it is a highly recognized symbol for having a business presence on the Internet.

.net represents the word "network," and is most commonly used by Internet service providers, Web-hosting companies or other businesses that are directly involved in the infrastructure of the Internet. Additionally, some businesses choose domain names with a .net extension for their intranet Websites.

.org represents the word "organization," and is primarily used by non-profits groups or trade associations.

.biz is used for small business Web sites.

.info is for credible resource Web sites and signifies a "resource" web site. It's the most popular extension beyond .com, .net and .org.
.mobi is one of the newest extensions and is primarily used for websites that are designed for mobile phones

.us is for American Web sites and is one of the newest extensions. It has the largest amount of available names in inventory.

.us.com is an alternate domain for the United States and is one of the newest extensions. It also has the highest available inventory.

.bz was originally designated as the country code for Belize, but is now commonly used by small business who can't get the name they want using the .biz extension. It is unrestricted and may be registered by anyone, from any country.

.tv is for rich content/multi-media Web sites, commonly used within the entertainment or media industry.

It is very important that you are 100% satisfied with your website name, domain name and extension. Once you have purchased your domain name or locked it up, YOU CANNOT GO BACK AND CHANGE IT. It is crucial that you understand this.

It has been my experience that if you purchase a website name that you are uncertain of or ho-hum about as your final choice, you will eventually end up hating it. Make sure of your name the first time! This will save you time and money in the long run.

FINDING A GOOD WEB HOST

FINDING A GOOD WEB HOST

IMPORTANCE :   VERY

COST: Approximately $60 / year
FREE options available

SUGGESTION: Writer's Top Choice – Best Web Host
www.IXWEBHOSTING.com

Now that we have a website & domain name picked out, we need to find a good web host. We will purchase our domain or url (www.YOURWEBSITE.com) from them directly. I have provided a list of 25+ free web hosts at the end of this chapter, to keep with our "FREE is better" theme.   However, I strongly recommend spending the $4 dollars a month here to gain access to the long list of upgrades provided in the "Key Features" section of this chapter. We shall definitely need those extra little features to build a website that runs programs, animated swish files and allows downloads. These will keep your customers coming back for more.

The FREE web hosts are typically for those individuals, not wanting to overdo it and keep their site pretty simple. Only about 20MB of personal web space, which is actually not too bad is offered. These site's have a lot of restrictions upon the user and typically try to sell additional upgrades to their web host plans to the customer. Although, it is a FREE route to begin getting your site up and running, be 100% sure if you want to go this route, it may end up costing you the same amount of money or more.....purchasing the upgrades that they offer.

What is a web host?

These are the questions you are probably asking yourself if you are new to the website building game. Web hosts are companies that provide space on a server or system they own for use by their clients as well as providing internet connectivity, typically in a data center. What this means to you is that, these companies will keep your website on the Internet continuously on their network and will give you access to make any modifications necessary to your website. The better Web Host Servers will also assist in getting you up and running, answer any questions and resolve any problem tickets you may post.

How to choose a web host?

There are literally hundreds, if not thousands of website's dedicated to selling web hosting services on the market today. How do we choose which is the best for our needs? Do some research and review on your own. You will most likely come across message boards or blogs with reviews from satisfied customer's claiming their web hosts are 'the best'. The most popular sites to discuss web hosts specifically are, HOSTSEARCH (www.hostsearch.com), TOPHOSTS (www.tophosts.com) and WEBHOSTDIR (www.webhostdir.com). A note of caution though, as with forums, a number of web hosts feel it is their duty to manipulate these options for their benefit and harm opposition. As the Web Editor of HostSearch.com, John Hughes suggests, 'It's a bottomless pit - some hosts change their IP addresses, use false email accounts - they do anything they can to manipulate reviews and ratings. It's a job keeping on top of it. The bottom line is that it doesn't matter how much effort goes into stopping this type of activity, there is no guarantee at the end of the day that bogus reviews aren't posted on web hosting sites. Although I am pretty sure most reviews on HostSearch.com are legitimate, some are cause for doubt. Be careful.

What should I look for?

Let's first think a little about the feature's we will need for our website. It is sort of like shopping for a car that you may be interested in purchasing. Will you need it for hauling? How many does it need to seat? Do you need a entertainment system in the back for the kids? Does it have power doors, windows, locks? Etc.

Important questions to think about when shopping for web host options…..

1. How much disk space do I need? A 10 page website may only need 100mb, but a 200 page site may require 2Gb+ to store all the pages.

2. How much bandwidth will I need?

3. Am I going to need access to extra utilities such as databases, chat rooms, forums, blogs or other medium where information can be stored and clients can connect with me?

4. Will I need to install and run special scripts and php applications (discussed in-depth in later chapters)?

5. What operating system should I run? Windows or Linux?

6. And the ultimate question, how much am I comfortable paying each month for these services?

Once you have answered these vital questions you are ready to begin your assessment of different web hosting providers. Let's look at these a little closer.

Disk Space

The amount of storage space the web host provider is giving you to store your website. Different plans will offer a variety of different storage options. If your website is already constructed you can generally determine how much storage space you will need by totaling the file sizes of your pages and images. An easier method would be to use the FREE tools that an internet website such as www.sitereportcard.com has to offer. Simply, log-on to their site and enter your url into the "ENTER URL" field. It will give you all kinds of relevant and interesting information about your website. To analyze our webpage size – click on the "LOAD TIME" option, once the site has finished its analysis. Should look something like this:

Total Page Size: 240.79 Kb.	**TOTAL PAGE SIZE**
Total objects on the site: 13	
HTML Page Size: 22.64 Kb.	**Your Website**
Images: 218.14 Kb.	
Rating: 1/10	**Your Total Image's**

Connection Speed	Download Time (sec)
14.4K	154.10
28.8K	77.05
56K	39.63
128K ISDN	17.34
1.44MB T1	1.61

The actual code for our site is only 22.64 kb. However, when we add in the 13 image files (218.14 kb) the total page size jumps up to 240.79 kb.
Repeat this step for any back pages you may have and add them up. That will tell you how much storage space you will need. It is always a good idea to attain more space than is necessary for additional pages that may be uploaded later.

Bandwidth

Your Bandwidth basically refers to the amount of data that can be transferred from your web site to the world. A measure for the speed (amount of data) you can send through an Internet connection. The more bandwidth, the faster the connection.

Let's assume that your home page, the first page served to your visitors, has a file size of 50 KB, 15 KB for the actual HTML page and 35 KB for images included on that page - backgrounds, buttons, logo, photos, etc.. Now let's also assume that your site gets 10,000 visitors per month and the average visitor views 3 pages of your site, also 50 KB each.

Based on those numbers, your site would serve: 50 KB x 3 Pages x 10,000 Visitors = 1500000 KB or 1500 MB or 1.5 GB per month.

Let's look at your data transfer based on server load. Assuming this traffic was evenly distributed, your server would be distributing 1.5 GB per month *<insert long math equation here>* or about 6 KB per second. At this rate your server is barely working. Let's assume that all of you visitors come to your site during the same hour of every day. Even then, the server load during this hour would only be 833 KB per second or less than 1 MB.

Other Upgrades & Utilities

Will you need to store dynamic information online about your products, services or clients? If so you'll want to be sure your plan provides a database tool. Databases are extremely versatile and will vary in flavor depending on the operating system you select for your hosting server.

In addition, there are a large variety of other upgrades and utilities that are offered when we choose the correct web host. Such items like : Blogs, CMS & Portals, Forums, E-Commerce, Support Systems, Galleries and more are easily downloaded at the click of a button.

KEY FEATURES

Let's compare some top web host's and find out which one will best suit our needs. I have done some research and found a few good sites to look into. They are:

- IXWEBHOSTING.COM   (writer's favorite)
- HOSTMONSTER.COM
- DREAMHOST.COM
- HOSTGATOR.COM
- BLUEHOST.COM

Now that you are armed with the proper tools for selecting your web host, compare the key factors that you want most from the web hosts I have provided (or go find one on your own). My intention is not to steer you toward anyone web host. I neither get a royalty or a commission from such a service. I only wish to eliminate the confusion and fear associated with the selection of a proper web host.

I am recommending IXWEBHOSTING.COM because I have personally had 5 website's running with them for the last five years and they have not let me down once. They are professional and very well educated in the assistance of any needs that you may have. From a "rookie" question to a very advanced problem, they have always come through for me. Just recently, I purchased the expert plan from them which only runs $3.95 a month (their most inexpensive plan) to work on a new site. Once confirmed I went off to work on other projects, knowing that it would take a day or two for my domain to propagate (go live into the world). After the third day, I realized that I misspelled the domain name wrong. What a mess, I thought to myself. I immediately called their support site and they fixed the problem, even though their policy on domain name changes was only 24 hours. In this day and age it is truly a rarity to find a company that values their customers the way they do.

.
IXWEBHOSTING.COM
Featured Domain Package Includes:

Host Multiple Domains	Unlimited
Disk Storage - NEW!	Unlimited
Free Domain Regs - Free For Life!*	2
Dedicated IP Addresses	8
Data Transfer - NEW!	Unlimited
Sub Domains	Unlimited
Free Site Builder - DEMO	✓
Free 24/7 Support	✓
Database Support	✓
Ecommerce Ready	✓

Email

🔍 Email Resources (Accounts)	**5,000**
🔍 Catch-All Email Addresses	✓
🔍 POP3	✓
🔍 IMAP	✓
🔍 Webmail	✓
🔍 Email Forwards	✓
🔍 Mailbox Aliases	✓
🔍 Email Auto-Responders	✓
🔍 Mailing Lists	✓
🔍 Total Mailbox Quota	**5 GB**

Scripting

🔍 PHP v5 - NEW	✓
🔍 Perl	✓
🔍 CGI with FastCGI support (only with Windows plans)	✓
🔍 CGI	✓
🔍 CGI-BIN	✓
🔍 ASP / ASP.NET v3.5 (only with Windows plans) - NEW	✓
🔍 Cold Fusion v7 MX (only with Windows plans) - NEW	✓
🔍 Javascript/DHTML	✓
🔍 Server Side Includes (SSI)	✓
🔍 Override .htaccess Support (only with Linux plans)	✓

Databases

🔍 MYSQL	**100**
🔍 PostgreSQL	**100**
🔍 Microsoft SQL 2005 (only with Windows plans) - NEW	**100**
🔍 ODBC/DSN (only with Windows plans)	✓
🔍 phpMyAdmin	✓
🔍 phpPgAdmin	✓
🔍 Total SQL Databases Quota	

Complimentary Scripts (NEW) COMPLETE LIST

- 🔍 Message Forum ✔
- 🔍 Blogs (Online Diaries) ✔
- 🔍 Photo Galleries ✔
- 🔍 Online Shops ✔
- 🔍 LiveChat System ✔
- 🔍 Web Portals and CMS ✔
- 🔍 Miscellaneous Scripts ✔

Ecommerce Features

- 🔍 Free Shared SSL Certificate ✔
- 🔍 SSL Secure Server ✔
- 🔍 Online Shop Ready ✔

Support Features

- 🔍 24/7 Free Live Phone Support ✔
- 🔍 24/7 Free LiveChat System ✔
- 🔍 24/7 Free Ticket Center ✔

Additional Features

- 🔍 International Domain Name Support ✔
- 🔍 Website Statistics ✔
- 🔍 Account Control Panel - DEMO ✔

File Transfer

- 🔍 FTP Access ✔
- 🔍 Additional FTP Accounts (Now Available in Windows!) ✔
- 🔍 Anonymous FTP Accounts ✔
- 🔍 FrontPage 2000/2002 Extensions ✔

Website Administration

- 🔍 FREE Professional Website Templates ✔
- 🔍 Create and Change Designs at Any Time ✔
- 🔍 Log Files + Site Stats ✔
- 🔍 Web File Manager ✔
- 🔍 Publishing Program ✔
- 🔍 Password Protected Directories (only with Linux plans) ✔
- 🔍 Online Web Editor ✔

- Custom MIME Types ✔
- Custom CRON Jobs (only with Linux plans) ✔
- Custom Error Pages ✔
- Custom Throttle Policy - NEW (only with Linux plans) ✔
- Custom Server Aliases - NEW ✔

Multimedia

- Flash & Shockwave Support ✔
- MIDI File Support ✔
- Streaming Audio Support (via http://) ✔
- Streaming Video Support (via http://) ✔
- Real Audio & Video Support ✔

Security Mechanism

- 24/7 Monitoring ✔
- Firewall Protection ✔
- Spam Filter Spam Assassin ✔
- UPS Power Back-up/Back-up Generator ✔
- Hotlink Protection ✔
- Server Load Balancing System ✔

Domain Management

- Domain Access with or without "www" ✔
- Domain Contact Management ✔
- External Domains ✔
- Parked Domains ✔
- URL Masking (only with Linux plans) ✔
- Add-on Domains

Please verify with IXWEBHOSTING.COM as this information was downloaded prior and may have changed**

The Good Web Hosting Providers will also give you an 'allowance' of FREE web marketing coupons to get your website up and running. Such as:

Google YAHOO!	FREE Advertisements Get $25 more with Unlimited Pro	**$350 Value Complete List**
SitePal	Your Own Speaking Character! Increase Sales To Your Site!	**$60 Value FREE Character**
website MAGAZINE practical ecommerce	Outdo Your Competitors! FREE Magazines for IX Customers!	**$48 Value FREE Magazines**

As this will be the majority of money spent on your website, it is vital that you get the most of your money. The above mentioned plan is available for $7.95 per month (2 year commitment) from

IXWEBHOSTING.COM. You can run Windows , Linux or

Mac OS on your computer without any problems

Using the above mentioned company is only a suggestion. They are an exceptional web host provider and have great backend website support. They are kind and courteous and use the latest technology to streamline the website building process.

Windows or Linux? What's the difference?

	Linux	Windows
Price	The majority of Linux variants are available for free or at a much lower price than Microsoft Windows.	Microsoft Windows are typically more expensive, however are free with most web hosts.
Ease	Windows is much easier to use for new computer users	Easier than Linux
Reliability	Notoriously Reliable and can run for months without needing to be rebooted	Cannot match the reliability of Linux
Software	Large Variety of	Larger selection of

	available software programs, however, cannot match Windows	available software, due to the large amount of Windows users
Security	Linux has always been a very secure operating system. Much more secure than Windows.	Windows operating system continues to be the most vulnerable to viruses and other attacks.
Support	More difficult system to operate.	Windows has its own help section and has vast amounts of online documentation

The difference between the two operating systems is a bit confusing. However, we recommend that new users use the Windows system (due to the ease of use). More advanced users may opt for the Linux oS, which is more secure. You may switch from one oS to the other if necessary (however, you may experience a downtime of approximately 12-24 hours) and will have to upload your website from A-Z.

Free Web Hosting for Your Personal Web Pages under 20mb

If you are not looking to publish a large site, there are also a number of Free Web Hosts for your personal web pages under 20mb. Most of these companies, have upgrade capabilities if you go over the 20mb.

NetFirms
Free hosting with Perl, CGI, SSI, and Flash capabilities. You can also get a free copy of NetObjects Fusion. 25MB, free domain hosting, FTP access, and email.
50megs.com
Get 12MB free, paid for with banner ads. And it's simple to pay just a little and get rid of the ads, and 50MB or more.
Angelfire Communications
Free advertising supported Web pages. 5MB storage.
BizLand.com
The Basic membership is free, but you don't get a lot, just a one-

page Web site "business card". But they also have a 30-day free trial of their next level of service.

Brinkster

Brinkster is an ASP information service, but if you join at the free "General Membership" level, you can post to their forums as well as get 30 MB free Web space with ASP support. One good thing about this service, there are no ads on your site, instead you agree to receive email ads.

The Burgh Network Solutions

This is a nice service as you get 20MB of ad free Web space. There is no FTP or CGI support.

Catalog.com

Catalog.com offers free Web hosting "forever" when you register a new domain with them or transfer your existing one to them.

Crosswinds

Crosswinds offers both free email and unlimited Web page hosting space.

dotEasy

This free hosting service has devised a new way to pay for their service. Instead of a banner ad on your site, you must agree to receive their newsletter. For this they offer: 20MB, free domain hosting, unlimited email addresses, FTP access, and more.

Dreamwater

50MB free, and you get guestbook, form email, clip art, and more. Plus it's free with no annoying pop-up ads.

EasySpace

25 MB of free Web space. It's easy to upgrade to more space for a low price.

Free Webspace.Net

If you are looking for a place to host your Web page for free, then Free Webspace.Net is the place to start. As of this writing they have 136 listings, and it can only go up.

Freeservers.com

You can have your name in your URL for free. Get 20MB free with this great hosting service.

FreeYellow

This service offers 20MB of free space, a wizard to help you create your pages, lots of graphics for your site, placement in the FreeYellow search engine, and best of all, it's free.

GeoCities

GeoCities is one of the first, and best known, Web hosting services on the Web. I had a GeoCities page for a long time.

Freedom2Surf

Frontpage 2000 support is a great feature on this free Web hosting provider. Plus you can get Perl CGI scripting access and PHP4. This is a free service suitable for more advanced developers.

Homestead

This is a free Web page builder where you don't need to know any HTML to create your page.

Hypermart

Hypermart will host business Web sites. The only "charge" is an advertisement is placed on your site.

MSN Communities

MSN uses TalkCity to help you create your Web pages quickly and easily.

Netfirms

This site gives you free 25MB of Web space, with no set up fee. It is paid for with an ad at the top of all your pages.

Netscape Site Central

Free Web hosting made simple

WebWowser

WebWowser offers an interesting service. You have to use their software to work on your site, but it's pretty easy to use. One caveat, your site must be updated regularly. If it is not, after 30 days of inactivity it will be taken down.

Spree

Spree is a shopping site that provides unlimited space free Web sites to its members.

Stormloader.com

25MB space with lots of tools to make it easy for you to make your Web page. Special features include free guest books, free message board, unlimited bandwidth, and free online support.

Tripod

Tripod divides the personal pages into categories and your site will be within one or more "pods" to facilitate searching.

XOOM.com

Xoom offers 11MB of free Web space. As they say, they will "always go the extra megabyte for you".

What I Collect Free Web Pages

If you're a collector you can host your site here, and get access to many community tools like forums, online libraries, and other things of interest to collectors.

Website hosting has become so affordable in today's market that it's not worth the aggravation a *FREE* service will put you through to utilize their resources. I tagged the word FREE because there's really no such thing as free web hosting providers.

Most free services are offered in exchange for placing ads or other annoying features automatically onto your website. Displaying ads on websites is a process that requires careful consideration – even when you are personally selling ad space on your own site. Placement of the ad, layout and content are all key factors in ensuring your ads do not drive away your target audience. When working with a free hosting service, most likely you do not have control over these items, and could not ensure that their ads would compliment your products and services. Far better to pay the $5 per month and secure reliable hosting that places no demands on your website than to select a *FREE* host and take your chances.

WEBSITE SETUP

IMPORTANCE: VERY
COST: FREE or Paid

Congratulations.   At this point, you have successfully chosen (locked) your website domain name (url). You are now the sole owner of your domain name. No one else on the planet may have the exact same name and extension. It is possible for another person to have the same name and different extension however.

> For example: www.yourwebsite.com is your website name and extension. It is possible to have another person use www.yourwebsite.net or www.yourwebsite.net.   It is important that you notice this aspect of website domain name selection. Two companies with the name ABC may exist. However, one is abc.com and the other is abc.net. Even though, these hypothetical companies may have nothing to do with each other, they are only separated by their extensions.

Is one extension better than the other? Ideally, you would assume that the ".com" extension is better, because it is more recognizable. The current trend for larger companies lately has been to use the ".org" extension when their first choice (".com extension") has been purchased by another party.

Let's imagine that a consumer/customer is searching for ABC company, and comes across multiple ABC companies in existence. How does the search engine (i.e. Google, Yahoo, etc.) determine the order of which company will be in the highest to lowest position. The ABC companies listed at the top of the list will obviously attract more traffic. There are a number of factors that Search Engines will look at when listing their search results. ABC.NET may have a better pagerank, alexa rank and more and better back-links to it's site along with having been established at an earlier time than ABC.COM. (We will discuss website ranking strategies later in the book). Even though the ".com" extension is more recognizable, the better traffic will go to ABC.NET.

ESSENTIAL TOOLS NEEDED TO BEGIN

- **Choosing a Web Editor – Different Types**

WYSIWYG Web Editors / Site Builders

A WYSIWYG (pronounced "wiz-ee-wig") editor or program is one that allows a developer to see what the end result will look like while the interface or document is being created. WYSIWYG is an acronym for "what you see is what you get". An HTML WYSIWYG editor conceals the markup and allows the Web page developer to think entirely in terms of how the content should appear. One of the trade-offs, however, is that an HTML WYSIWYG editor sometimes inserts the markup code it thinks is needed all on its own. Then, the developer has to know enough about the markup language to go back into the source code and clean it up.

Free HTML Editors / Free PHP/Perl/JavaScript (etc) Editors

For more advanced users, HTML editors have a greater emphasis on the coding of the web pages. They are basically ASCII text editors with additional features that make it easier for you to write and edit the HTML code for the website page. Very often, this includes syntax highlighting for the HTML/CSS elements (and perhaps also for PHP, Perl, JavaScript, ASP, Java elements as well). If you write your pages using raw HTML, or if you plan to learn to write HTML, these are the editors you will want to check.

- **Free vs. Paid Web Editor's**

Now that we know what the different types of editor's do, we have to decide on using a FREE web editor versus one we purchase. For all intents and purposes, a FREE web editor will be the first choice that comes to everyone's mind initially, but we must consider the additional features and upgrades that come with purchasing a good web editor. It is essential that everyone, beginning to advanced webmaster, be entirely comfortable with their choice of web editor. For most, this will be the primary tool used in the construction and maintenance of your web pages for your website. Do not settle for a web editor that is too simple, or attempt to use one that is too complex. Choose one that compliments your understanding and aptitude of basic computer language and syntax. If you are new to the web building game but have an eagerness to learn you will do just fine. There will always be a bit of a learning curve with any new software you are using, WYSIWYG or HTML Editor. Keep at it and don't be afraid to try new things. ALWAYS BACKUP YOUR SITE. It's a good idea to backup your backup as well.

There are many HTML editor's to choose from. Since we are attempting to build your website with the minimal amount of cost, lets find some FREE one's first. There are a ton of FREE editor's to choose from. In your address bar, type in 'FREE HTML EDITORS AND WYSIWYG WEB EDITORS'. Do a little research and experiment with the one that is most comfortable to use.

FREE WEB EDITOR'S

A great FREE web editor (ranked highly) is **Nvu 1.0** (http://www.nvu.com/index.php). Pronounced "N-view," Nvu 1.0 is a complete, although very basic web design solution for Windows, Mac and Linux that is 100% free, available to anyone for download. Based on Mozilla Composer, Nvu 1.0 lets users create quick and easy websites, without having to know HTML. The software still includes some more advanced bells and whistles like JavaScript coding and CSS support. Tech support and documentation is a common weakness of freeware, and reviews found Nvu thin in this area, though there is a forum for posting questions to other users.

Another outstanding FREE web editor (award winning) is PageBreeze www.pagebreeze.com. PageBreeze Free HTML Editor's design emphasizes simplicity and ease-of-use. It uses a mix of both HTML editor and WYSIWYG modes. Has a low learning curve and is recommended for beginning webmasters. Emphasis on drag and drop technology, latest form building techniques and 100's of FREE website templates to get your site up and running quickly.

For additional FREE web editors go to: http://www.thefreecountry.com/webmaster/htmleditors.shtml

I recommend that all beginning webmasters choose a WYSIWYG web editor. No reason to get hung up on all the technicalities of HTML code scripting if you don't need to. As stated earlier, WYSIWYG is an acronym for 'What You See Is What You Get'. Stated very plainly: a system in which content displayed during editing appears very similar to the final output. Very simple and straightforward. Minimal HTML programming required. Most of us have the Microsoft Office uploaded onto our computers and with that application comes Microsoft's Frontpage web editor. This is more than enough when attempting to build simple web pages. When I say simple, I do not want you to think that the website will look bad. Not at all. More expensive applications like Dreamweaver for example, are for experienced webmaster's who can use all the extensive feature's available. Dreamweaver is also a bit pricey for the beginning webmaster.

TOP PAID & FREE EDITORS
About.com 1 Year Reviews

☐ **TextPad version 5.2**   ★★★★★

   http://www.textpad.com

- Price Paid: Free with purchase
- Type of Web Editor: I don't know
- Operating System: Windows, Macintosh, Linux

   "TextPad is a free to try, $32 USD to buy. This is a small price for such a vast amount of usability."

☐ Aptana version 0.2.7.1342 ★★★★★

http://www.aptana.com

- Price Paid: Free
- Type of Web Editor: Text
- Operating System: Windows

"All in all, I like Aptana."

☐ Boxer Text Editor version 13.0.0.0 ★★★★★

http://www.boxersoftware.com

- Price Paid: $26-$50
- Type of Web Editor: Text
- Operating System: Windows

"You can create your own space within it - just the way you want it to look. I also replaced Notepad with Boxer."

☐ Serif Web Plus 10 version 10.0 ★★★★★

http://www.serif.com/webplus

- Price Paid: $26-$50
- Type of Web Editor: WYSIWYG
- Operating System: Windows

"If you're just getting started, but want to look pro, this program is the easiest one I found."

☐ Macromedia Dreamweaver version MX2004 ★★★★★

http://www.adobe.com/products/dreamweaver/

- Price Paid: $101-$500
- Type of Web Editor: WYSIWYG, Text

- Operating System: Windows, Linux

"I found it easy to get to grips with and, as my capabilities grew, I found that the software was able to meet all my growing requirements."
Dreamweaver Help and Resources

CONNECTING TO OUR WEBSITE

- **Understanding FTP or File Transfer Protocol**

What is it? FTP or File Transfer Protocol is used to transfer files between computers on a network, such as the Internet. You can use FTP to exchange files between computer accounts, to transfer files between an account and a desktop computer, or to access software archives on the Internet. Keep in mind, however, that many FTP sites are heavily used and require several attempts before connecting.

Any good web editor will come with FTP upload / publish capabilities built into the software. It is not a bad idea to have a secondary means of accessing your site also.

FREE FTP CLIENT SOFTWARE

CORE FTP
http://www.coreftp.com/download.html

FREE Windows software that includes features like SFTP (SSH), SSL, TLS, IDN, browser integration, site to site transfers, FTP transfer resume and more. A fast, easy and reliable way to update and maintain your website.

WALKTHROUGH

- **First time connecting to our website - Setup**

Time to setup your Website Editor. Open your editor and press the connect or publish button. This will take you to the publish window (seen below). The left side of the screen shows the files on your computer, as well as, which files are open. The right side of the screen WILL show you your website files, once connected. When not connected to your site , the right side of the screen will be blank. NOT connected to your site, the image should look something like the example below:

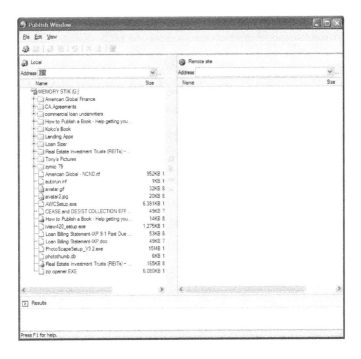

Press the connect button. We will next need to ADD our site. This will open the remote site settings window. In the fields, we will enter all our critical information – allowing us to connect to our site. Now we will setup our connection from our computer to our web hosts server, so that we may transfer files back and forth, to and from our website.

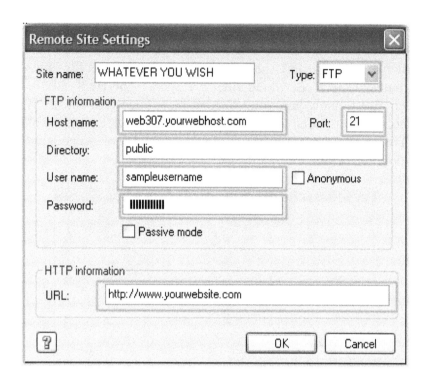

The most important information to log onto your website is the FTP information & HTTP information here (highlighted areas). All this information is readily available by logging into your Web Host Provider. After logging into your control panel via your web host, access your FTP manager or control panel. The FTP manager will have all the above needed information. Your Login, Password (you may change here if needed), Home Directory location, Host Name along with a few other stats.

If your have any problems connecting to your site, feel free to call your web host directly with any questions they may have. They may be a bit technical, but keep asking until you are comfortable you have the correct information. They are there to help you, don't forget that.

Once you have all the information correct and click on that connect button, you should begin to see files on the right side of the screen. You have successfully connected to your website. Congratulations. You will see a few file folders in the right column along with an

INDEX.HTML file and maybe a .gif or .jpg file also. Image names may vary from host to host.

To clarify: You are now successfully connected to your website. The files you are looking at are the default homepage setup by your web host indicating that your website is under construction. The image files (.jpg / .gif) are exactly what they seem to be...pictures. To clarify, go to your website via the internet. Type in your website name, i.e. www.mywebsite.com.

In order to notify you that your site is up and running, your web host provider has set up a default 'website under construction' page. Or else you would be looking at a totally blank screen, because, you haven't uploaded anything onto your site yet. The web host posts the identical default home page for all new sites. The files are very basic and easily removed. These files usually are very simple and consist of a INDEX.HTML file and some picture (jpg or gif) files. You can leave these here for now, or delete them. Be careful to only delete the index.html file and/or any jpy or gif files that may be visible. DO NOT DELETE ANY FOLDERS! They contain important site programs that you will need. If you do, just call your web host server directly and ask them to re-install your site from scratch.

Your Homepage / INDEX File

What is a homepage / index file? Your homepage is your top page on your website. When a customer types in www.yourwebsite.com in attempts to find your site, this is what will come up. In actuality, when entering yourwebsite.com, the search engine is actually looking for yourwebsite.com/index.html.

The INDEX file is the primary file that will be called upon when search engines find your site. All traffic will be channeled through this FRONT PAGE (to keep it simple, there are ways to redirect traffic if needed). You may only need a few pages on your entire website or maybe you are constructing a vast database and need thousands of pages, it all starts with your homepage.

INDEX.HTML is the (primary) default homepage file

It is important to note that HTML (HyperText Markup Language) is not the only extension available for storing your web pages. Without being too technical, there are alternate file extension. HTML or HTM. HTML files originated with Unix, where Web pages are commonly identified with an .HTML extension. The .HTM is an alternate in the Windows world, because three-byte extensions (.EXE, .DOC, etc.) are so commonly used.

It is possible to have .html files and .htm files working on your website at the same time, as long as there are links pointing to each file and extension. Both extension types work exactly the same:

Index.html	Index.htm
Index.html/mywebsite.html	Index.htm/mywebsite.htm
Practice.html	Practice.htm
Test.html	Test.htm

Concentrate on only using one type of file extension and stick to it. The more you combine the two types the more confusion will arise. Our website should be clean, clear and transparent to us, as webmasters. One look at your websites files should be all you need to sniff out any errors that may be present. By introducing two types of extensions in our website, may be confusing and difficult to discern any errors that may be present.

What if no index.html file exists? Search engines will search your site in attempts of locating a homepage in a systematic method. If no INDEX.HTML file is present then INDEX.HTM will automatically become your default homepage. If there is no index.htm file then INDEX.PHP file will automatically become your default homepage and etc.

The PHP extension is a computer scripting language, typically used to produce dynamic web pages. We'll discuss this language in depth later in the book.

Our First Test – Initial Upload To Our Website

Now that we understand where everything is, let's begin our first test. In order to continue, let's establish a folder on your computer (probably on your C: drive) named My Website or something to that affect. This way, you may save and extrapolate files in one concentrated area.

Now that you have your folder setup, the next step is to open your web editor software (not necessary to connect to your website yet). Next step, Open a blank page. Type in some text here, doesn't matter what it is. Now save this file as TEST. Your editor will save it as test.html or test.htm. Now upload to your site.

Connect to your website / Publish this page, should look like this:

Since we have not changed the location of the default homepage or index.html on the web host server, yourwebsite.com will look exactly the same as before. In order to access or bring up the page we just uploaded, let's type in http://www.yourwebsite.com/test.html or http://www.yourwebsite.com/test.htm depending on what you named the test page and what the extension is. You should now see the exact page you uploaded on your screen.

Second Test – Uploading an Image

Repeat the beginning steps as before. Open your web editor. Open a blank page. Rename the page to IMAGETEST.HTML (only type in IMAGETEST, the html extension tag is automatic). Now comes the fun part of this test, let's find some images on the internet and save them to our website folder. For example: lets go to Google's Image / Picture Site (http://www.images.google.com). In the address bar, type in 'Under Construction'. Point your cursor over any image and right click on the mouse. This will give you the option of how you would like to save the image. Use the 'Save Image As' and 'Name' options.

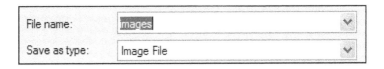

Make sure to save the file into your "WEBSITE FILE", so you can find it later when you need to work with it. You may rename the image to anything you would like – make sure it has some relevance to you, so that you may call upon the image and be certain of what it is (without opening it up) later. For example, if a file is a construction image, then we will call it construction.jpg or something to that effect. Remember, it is not necessary to enter the extensions. The default settings will take over if no preference is made.

Now that you have an image saved to your folder, let's go back to the web editor. On another blank screen, let's use the "INSERT IMAGE" option from your tool bar. Double click on the image file you just downloaded and renamed to add it to your webpage. Next, Name and Save the webpage. Next publish / upload to your website. Now let's go see if the webpage and image we published is there.

Now just as before, go to your internet connection and open up your website again. Type in your http://www.websitename.com/imagetest.html. You should be looking at a blank screen with an EMPTY BOX where your image should be. Don't panic, this is normal.

The image is not there because we have only saved and uploaded the webpage and not the image. It is important that you know why your image(s) are not showing up on your site.

Everything looked fine on my site in my web editor / offline. But when I upload to my website, the images do now show up. Why?

This is an easy fix and happens to everyone.

Right click on the box where your image should be. Look at the PROPERTIES. This should read www.yourwebsite.com/imagetest.html.

It is critical that we identify and resolve image errors quickly. An easy way to fix the problem is to right click on the box where the image is supposed to be. Now look at the location / address. This will tell you where the web browser is searching for that image. When it can't find the image at the location / address, it puts up the default image error box.

What has happened is the web page (IMAGETEST.HTML) is searching for the 'under construction' image and cannot find it on your web host. We need to go back and upload the image also into the correct folder.

In the following example, the web host is looking for the images / html files in the root or top level of the website.

www.yourwebsite.com/imagetest.html
Image is in the top level of your website

The web host is looking for the image / html files in the secondary level of the website. In the images folder.

www.yourwebsite.com/images/imagetest.html
Image is in the IMAGES folder

You may use this procedure in identifying any and all 'blank' images that we forgot to upload to your our website. Make sure the LOCATION and NAME of the file match exactly to what the website page is searching for.

Let's go back to your web editor. Open up your connection to your website via the publish option. Once you have your 'live' link with your website, publish the image (upload the image file) to your website. Go back to your website and open the imagetest.html page. Your image should be viewable now. If not, review this procedure and repeat process.

Upload html file and image file simultaneously!

SETTING UP YOUR WEB EDITOR CORRECTLY

SETTING UP YOUR WEB EDITOR CORRECTLY

It is important before we begin designing / building our website that we setup our web editor correctly. Many web editors have hundreds, if not thousands of options / tools at our disposal in creating websites. DO NOT GET DISTRACTED. You may look at the primary web editing screen and be overwhelmed as to where to begin. You might even say to yourself, 'I can't do this'. You couldn't be more wrong. Spend a little bit of time getting familiar with your editor. Not all editors are the same, and it is important you get a good idea of what you will need and when.

The easiest way to begin is to minimize all the 'noise' (window on the left side, bottom & right side) of your blank screen. Even though these items are placed to help us facilitate website building, they may just get in the way. Most, if not all, of the functions needed are listed at the top of the page in the toolbars.

Initial Web Editor Setup

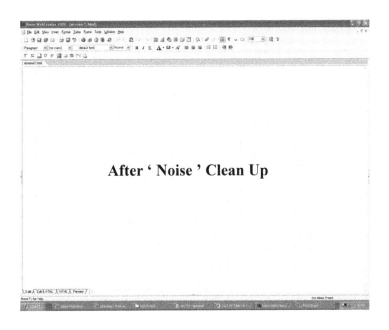

After ' Noise ' Clean Up

All the items we have minimized are all available from the toolbars located on top of the page. We can now view a larger area of our web page to edit.

The toolbars that will be used most and should be listed on top of your page are:

- Standard Toolbar

New Page / Save As / Save / Save All / Send E-mail / Print / Spell Check   Publish / View in Internet Explorer / Copy & Paste / Undo & Redo / Insert Image / Insert Flash Buttons / Create Table / Insert Layer / Split Frames / Hyperlink / Show & Hide Gridlines / Show & Hide Paragraph Marks / Show & Hide Space Marks / Show & Hide Special Tag Marks / Zoom In & Out / Help

- Formatting Toolbar

Paragraph Set Up / Class / Fonts / Size / Bold / Italics / Underline / Font Color / Text Background Color / Clear Character Format / Align Left / Align Center / Align Right / Numbered List / Bulleted List / Decrease Indent / Increase Indent

There are a number of other lists that are available. However, these other toolbars may be opened and closed when necessary.

Other toolbars available are:

- Form Toolbar (Used when setting up web forms).

A web form is placed on a web page and allows a user to enter data that is sent to a server for processing. It is primarily used to eliminate paper forms and facilitate the interaction of the user and the server. Forms can also be used to submit data to save on a server, such as ordering a product. Forms can also be used to retrieve data, such as searching for a specific item on a search engine. Forms will be discussed in full in later chapters.

- Hyperlink Toolbar (Used in setting up navigation to and from a website page)

A hyperlink is a reference or navigation element on a web page to another section of the same website or page and or to another domain (website). This link provides direct access from one distinctively marked place to another. Its function is to allow the reader / user to explore interesting links to other web pages linked to specific words or images within a page. Hyperlinks will be discussed in full in the following chapters.

- Image Toolbar

Pictures / Images are inserted into web pages. Create photo albums, insert clipart, insert flash images. Modification of image size, quality, format etc. Images will be discussed in full in the following chapters.

- Table Toolbar

A table is a set of data elements (values) that is organized using a model of vertical and horizontal columns. These columns may be identified by their name. These tables have a specific number of columns, but can have any number of rows. Each row is identified by the values appearing in a particular column.

Tables may also be used to set up simple websites. Using their simple box configuration, the addition and/or subtraction of cells is quite easy.

HTML BASICS

Before beginning to our web page design strategy, it is important that we understand some basic HTML terminology. Many, if not all web editors have a PREVIEW screen (what the page will look like when published), a EDIT screen (which allows for click & drop / cut & paste editing), some type of EDIT/HTML mix (showing simple editing and its HTML language associated with) and HTML only format (which shows the Hypertext Markup Language).

Hypertext Markup Language, what is it?

By now, you've heard about HTML or hypertext markup language. It is a process of taking ordinary text and adding extra symbols. These symbols tell the web browser how to display the text. Simply stated, the markup languages are computer languages that are solely concerned with classifying a web document according to their functions. For example: which part of the web page is governing the title or 'header' of the document, which part is the 'meat' or relevant middle part of the document, and which part is the bottom or 'footer' of the document.

Some basic HTML terms you will run into:

- **<html></html>**---begins and ends web document, tells the browser that the document is in HTML
- **<head></head>**---header, used after html tag
- **<title></title>**---located within header container
- **<body></body>**---creates the body of the document body attributes---to be used within <body> tag
- **background**="sample.jpg"---background picture
- **bgcolor**="color"---background color
- **text**="color"---text color

- **alink**="color"---active link color
- **vlink**="color"---visited link
- **bgproperties**---when equal to "fixed", background does not scroll
- **topmargin**---sets height of top margin
- **leftmargin**---sets width of left margin(not used in Netscape)

Document Formatting Tags

- **<p>**---place at the end of a paragraph, it will then skip a line for the next paragraph
- **<align=left, right, center></align>**---alignment
- **
**---line break, it will begin again on the next line
- **<nobr></nobr>**---no line breaks are allowed to occur within the container (be careful)
- **<wbr>**---gives the browser suggestions for where a break should occur if needed, use within the <nobr> tag
- **<h1></h1>**---heading style, choose from sizes 1(largest)-6(smallest)
- **<hr>**---horizontal line horizontal line attributes--- to be used within the <hr> tag
- **align=left, right, center**---alignment
  width=---in percentages or pixels
  size=---thickness, in pixels
  noshade---keeps browser from using 3D effects on line
  color="color"---line color
- **<pre></pre>**---for preformatted text, comes up as monospaced
- **&lt and &gt**---represent < and > without the functionality, so you can display them without being interpreted as commands

Text Formatting Tags

- **<i></i>**---italics
- **<b></b>**---bold
- **<u></u>**---underline
- **<tt></tt>**---teletype, monospaced text

- **<blockquote></blockquote>**---formatted for quoted text
- **<strike></strike>**---strikethrough style
- **<big></big>**---bigger text
- **<small></small>**---smaller text
- ****---subscript
- ****---superscript
- **<font face="font name"></font>**---to select specific font
- **<font size=1></font>**---font size, sizes 1-7
- **<font color="color"></font>**---font color
- **<base font>**---the font for the document, can use face, size and color with it

Graphics Formatting Tags

- **<img src="filename">**---Places an image within your document, review relative vs. absolute links. image attributes
- **align=top,middle,bottom**---align text with picture's top, middle, or bottom
- **align=left,right**---place picture on left or right and wrap text around it
- **width,height=**---in pixels or percentage, dimensions of picture can be altered (be careful with the ratio if using pixels)
- **alt=**---description of the picture so that text-only browsers know what it is
- **border=**---in pixels, border around the picture
- **vspace,hspace=**---in pixels, empty space around picture

Linking Tags

- **<a href="http://serendip.brynmawr.com/text.html">text link</a>**---text link, absolute link
- **<a href="text.html">text link</a>**---text link, relative link
- **<base href="http://serendip.brynmawr.com">**---gives web site for all relative links

- **<a href="http://serendip.brynmawr.com"><img src="sample.jpg"></a>**---graphic link
- **<a name=middle>middle section of web page</a>**---internal anchor
- **<a href="#middle">jump tp the middle</a>**---link to the internal anchor
- **<a href="mailto:me@serendip.brynmawr.edu"></a>**---link to email
- **<a href="news:news.newuser.questions"></a>**---link to Usenet group
- **<a href="ftp://ftp.mysite.com/pub/FAQ"></a>**---link to ftp
- **<a href="gopher://gopher.mysite.com"></a>**---link to gopher site

Tables

- **<table></table>**---table tag Table attributes---all of which can refer to the whole table or single cell (by using <th>, <td>, <tr>)
- **border=**---in pixels
- **align=left, right, center**---alignment of data within the cells
- **valign=top, middle, bottom**---vertical alignment of data within the cells
- **width/height=**---in pixels, of table or individual cells
- **cellpadding/cellspacing=**---in pixels, adds space within cell/border
  bordercolor/bgcolor="color"---will change table, row, or cell border/background color, use with td, th, and tr tags
- **rowspan/colspan**---allows one cell to occupy more than one "cellblock"
- **<th></th>**---table header within the cells-can use valign=top/middle/bottom and align=left/right/center
- **<td></td>**---table data within the cells-can use valign=top/middle/bottom and align=left/right/center
- **<tr></tr>**---table row
- **<caption></caption>**---places a caption, either above or below <table align=top/bottom>

- ---keep in mind that you can place a picture in a table by using <img src...> between <td>...</td>
Hexadecimal Color System

Black	#000000	Maroon	#800000	Green	#008000	Olive	#808000
Navy	#000080	Purple	#800080	Teal	#008080	Gray	#808080
Silver	#C0C0C0	Red	#FF0000	Lime	#00FF00	Yellow	#FFFF00
Blue	#0000FF	Fuchsia	#FF00FF	Aqua	#00FFFF	White	#FFFFFF

Frames

- **<frameset></frameset>**---to designate use of frames, but will be ignored if <body> tag is present Frameset Attributes---found within the <frameset> tag
- **rows/cols=**---in pixels/percentages/proportions, pixels set an absolute distance while the other two give relative distances
- ---proportions are designated by *,2*,*;which is 1/4,1/2,1/4
- **border=**---in pixels, assigns a width to all frames
- **frameborder=yes,no**---default is yes for a 3-D look, no turns off the effect
- **bordercolor="color"**---defines color for all frame borders
- **<frame>**---defines each individual frame, and there must be one per created frame Frame Attributes---found within the <frame> tag
- **src=**---must use URL of either a HTML document or picture, text alone can not be used
- **name=**---assigned to each frame so that they can be linked to from other frames
- **target=**---it designates which frame a new link will be opened up within when used in the <a href> tag
- ---for example, <a href="list.html" target="one"> will open *list.html* in frame *one*
- ---can also be used to name windows
- **="_blank"**---will launch a new browser window with the link's contents

- **="_self"**---will replace the frame with the link's contents
- **="_parent"**---the frameset will be replaced by link's contents
- **="_top"**---replaces current browser window with link's contents
- **scrolling=yes,no,auto**---auto is the default, but the scrollbars can be turned on or off when possible
- **marginwidth/height=**---in pixels, area within border where source content will not be shown
- **noresize**---prevents users from resizing individual and adjacent frames, in order to preserve layout
- **bordercolor="color"**---defines color for individual frame border
- **<noframes></noframes>**---use this tag to provide alternate content for those with non-frames compatible browsers
- ---can safely use the <body> tag with it's attributes within this container
- **note**---one can place frames(<frameset>) within frames(<frameset>) to create more complex layouts

These are some basic HTML tags you will run into. There is a vast amount of information on the HTML or Hypertext Markup Language both published and on the internet. These basic classes listed above touch lightly on these areas. They are provided to give the first time webmaster insight as to how HTML tags work. Also, each of the five types of tags will be used by ALL webmasters, beginner's and masters alike.

BRAND NEW WEB PAGE viewed via HTML

```
1 <html>
2
3 <head>
4 <title>No title</title>
5 </head>
6
7 <body bgcolor="white" text="black" link="blue" vlink="purple" alink="red">
8 <p> </p>
9 </body>
10
11 </html>
```

The Published or Preview of the screen is blank

Entering Some Text – 'Hello World'

```
1 <html>
2
3 <head>
4 <title>No title</title>
5 <meta name="generator" content="Namo WebEditor">
6 </head>
7
8 <body bgcolor="white" text="black" link="#0099FF" vlink="purple" alink="red">
9 <p>Hello World</p>
10 </body>
11
12 </html>
```

The Published or Preview of screen

Hello World

INITIAL WEB DESIGN

Now that you are armed with some website building basics, we are ready to jump into our initial web design. But before we do, it is important that you be ready for the bombardment of solicitations that you will no doubt be subject to in building your website. Companies promising they can design and build your website for almost nothing, others will offer you free website services and seo promotion tools.

YOU DON'T NEED ANY OF THEM! You can do it all on your own, if you have the drive and the passion to create something out of nothing. Better yet, doing it all for FREE!

Back to website building......I like to think of the initial blank screen as our canvas and we are the painters. A web page can be anything you would like it to be. You are only limited by your imagination, as to its configuration and setup. Your website homepage may be simplistic, or very complex. There is no right or wrong layout, however there are some basic website formats to consider.

Remember, your homepage is the most important webpage on your website. In most cases, it is the first (and last) thing people will see when they click on your site. To entice them to dig deeper into your website, this first impression is crucial.

Let's look at a few examples of successful website's and their layout. You may recognize the homepage for Google – It is a very simple and basic layout.

Even though this homepage is very basic, it is the gateway to approximately 150 millions hits daily. Simple is not always simple. The most popular search engine on the planet was started by two college students, Sergey Brin and Larry Page, with a $100k cheque in their pockets.

Let's look at an example of a very complex homepage. YAHOO

This web page has tons of information to click through. It has multiple RSS Feeds (discussed later) and constantly updated to keep information fresh up to the minute. You may click into your email, view the weather in your area, read an current article or read up on your favorite TV show. Teams of individuals are responsible for this top website.

BASIC WEBSITE FORMATS

The following list of website format's is provided to help give you some ideas of how you would like your website to look.

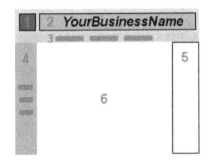

1. Your Logo
2. Banner – Business Name
3. Horizontal Menu
4. Vertical Menu
5. Hot Links
6. Body

This is a very basic web layout. The positions of the logo and banner can be interchanged. The body can be single or multi-column. The menu can be vertical or horizontal. The Hot Links column can also be added to the body area if required. Obviously, you can change the colors and textures provided.

HOME PAGE, VERTICAL MENU EXAMPLE

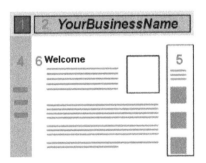

In this example, the menu or 3 from the list above has been taken out. The menu is listed solely on the left column or number 4.

ONE COLUMN LAYOUT

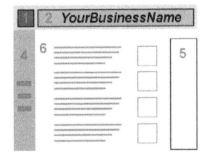

In this example, the website is ready for products / services which are best accompanied by a graphic, or where several lines of text are required for description.

Also, very useful for one-line lists (Product Description, Price) with alternate lines highlighted for ease of use.

TWO COLUMN LAYOUT

In this example, useful for displaying items effectively which do not require much text, and provides an attractive display for a large number of items.

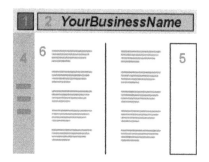

THREE COLUMN LAYOUT

In this example, the three column's demonstrate the full width of the page by utilizing a horizontal menu. The body contains examples of text items, and bordered boxes which may contain text or graphics or a mixture of both.

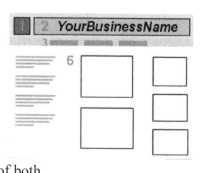

CONTACTS PAGE

This page will contain your Business Name & Address details, with e-mail addresses for your individual contacts. We can

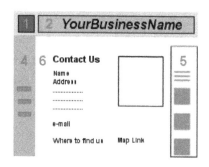

also add graphics of your Business Premises, photographs of your chief contacts, and a link to map site so that your customers can visit you in person if you wish this.

These basic formats may be seen all throughout the internet. These formats are only suggestions. As stated previously, the webpage design process is like a 'blank canvas'. You should feel free artistically. There is no 'CORRECT" method to website design. Consumers and customers surfing the internet are use to these design formats. However, you are not limited to any constraints when designing your website layout.

YOUR LOGO

As is the nature of the business of web design, someone will always try to sell you something you don't need. Running a search for 'web logo design' will bring you countless companies offering to sell you your own personal logo, custom designed to your specifications for a small fee. Not necessary. You are more than capable of designing your company logo for FREE.

Search the internet for company logo's for your specific website category. For example, real estate, healthcare, financial services, etc. Get an idea from these, to inspire you to make your own.

Listed below are just a few FREE picture / image editors that will allow you to do this:

- PHOTOSCAPE – Download from Cnet

  PhotoScape is an all-in-one style photo editor with fun and ease of use. Major capabilities are: viewer, editor, batch editor, page, combine, animated GIF, print, splitter, screen capture, color picker, rename, raw converter, resizing, brightness/color/white-balance adjustment, backlight correction, frames, balloons, text, drawing pictures, cropping, filters, red eye removal and blooming. PhotoScape has been used for two years and is expanding its features continuously.

- VICMAN'S PHOTO EDITOR – Download from www.vicman.net

VCW VicMan's Photo Editor is a versatile image editor with an intuitive interface. This award-winning application is free of charge and comes with a wide range of essential features for both novice users and professional designers. With Photo Editor you can refine your digital photos, draw natural artwork and effortlessly produce superb graphics for the web.

- COOLTEXT.COM – Visit Website

Cool Text is a free graphics generator for web pages and anywhere else you need an impressive logo without a lot of design work. Simply choose what kind of image you would like. Then fill out a form and you'll have your own custom image created on the fly in seconds.

- INFRANVIEW 4.2 – Download From Cnet

IrfanView is a fast and compact image viewer/converter. It is trying to be simple for beginners and powerful for professionals. Many supported file formats and features. Features include: multi-language support, Thumbnail option, Painting, slideshow, toolbar skins, fast directory browsing, batch conversion/editing, multipage editing, file search, change color depth, scanning, cut/crop, IPTC edit, capturing, lossless JPG operations, effects, ICC support, EXE/SCR creating, many hotkeys, command line options and plugins.

YOUR BANNER

Designing your banner is important, because that is the first image that visitors to your website will see. First impressions are everything. There are many site's willing to sell you a nice banner. Why would we go that route when we can get one for FREE. Below are a few FREE banner's I have downloaded that look great.

Banner's come in different shapes. Usually a LEADERBOARD or Full Banner is 728 x 90 pixels. A BANNER is 468 x 60 in dimension.

TIPS TO CUSTOMIZE LEADERBOARDS AND BANNERS

In order to make these leaderboards and banners specifically customized for your website, a few slight modifications may be necessary. We will need to first erase the default company name.

- Customizing Our Website Banner

Let's take the banner below for example:

This is a typical banner for a movie rental website. I have chosen this particular banner because the company name and backdrop are very easy to alter. The default name of the company given is www.companyname.com in the top left corner of the banner.

The next step – let's open the image with one of our FREE image editors. In the following example, I will alter the Image using Vicman's Photo Editor. The screen shot below is my image loaded onto Vicman's Software (also zoomed into the area we are going to alter).

Now that our image is loaded and we have zoomed into the area for modification lets use the eyedropper function on the top left of the screen to capture the exact color of the area behind the www.companyname.com. This will enable us to completely erase the default name.

Once we have the background color locked. Let's go ahead and begin painting over the default company name using the brush option. As you can see, it begins erasing the name completely.

Once we have erased the default title of the banner completely the rest is simple. Select the Front, Color and Size of your company name. You may need to make a few passes to get it right. Feel free to use the 'Go Back' button before you save the image.

I have named our sample banner WWW.WIDGETS.COM. Save and store our modified banner into our website folder. Always use the highest quality image format - 100%. You will be using this banner on ALL your webpage's from here on. It is a good idea to back up this image and store it somewhere safe as well. The finished product looks like this.

There are many FREE banner template website's to choose from. I shall list a few in the following chapter FREE TEMPLATES. You can use techniques similar to that shown above along with cut and paste strategies to dissect a few banners of your liking and combining the finished product into one unique banner – Your Very Own.

HORIZONTAL & VERTICAL (NAVIGATION) MENU'S

A Horizontal Menu facilitates the navigation on a web site by a collection of links. It is important to list only those links that are vitally essential to the entire website. For example, looking at a website that is based on consumer shopping, the navigation bar has the following look:

Listed under the company logo and banner, this horizontal menu will be consistently located in exactly the same place throughout the entire website (which may be thousands of pages deep). Customers will always know where the primary category buttons are located to speed up the search for the merchandise they are looking to buy.

Accessories
Baby & Toddler Accessories
Baby & Toddler Clothes
Handbags & Luggage
Kids
Kids' Accessories
Kids' Clothes
Maternity Clothes
Men's
Men's Accessories
Men's Activewear
Men's Clothing
Specialty Apparel
Women's
Women's Accessories
Women's Activewear
Women's Clothing
Women's Lingerie

Vertical Menu's differ from Horizontal Menu's in that they are constantly changing from web site page to web site page depending on the subject material.

These are secondary links to different pages throughout your web site that you would like to direct traffic to. In this example, we are using a vertical menu from a large retail company. Their vertical menu set up allows the visitor to quickly pick and choose which categories they desire.

SETTING UP YOUR MENU BUTTONS

Initially, pick your menu style you want to use. You may choose either, simple text or insert a button. Buttons are like small images / pictures. FREE buttons are available all over the internet. Customizing each button specifically for your website is the ideal choice for better web site look and feel.

COOLTEXT
http://www.cooltext.com
is one of the best FREE button makers available. Make a few or a thousand. No charge. Choose from an almost infinite number of possible textures, colors, fonts and sizes.

FREEBITS
http://www.freebits.co.uk/menubar.html
FREE web button and navigation button construction for your website. Examples for making simple or advanced menu bars to give your web page that something extra.

SCRIPTOCEAN.COM
http://www.scriptocean.com/drop-down-menu.html
Offering downloadable software which will allow you to design your FLASH based dropdown menu in a matte of minutes. The program gives you complete control over the appearance of your menu's.

LISTAMATIC
http://css.maxdesign.com.au/listamatic/
All types of styles and HTML script for altering and modifying your CSS (Cascading Style Sheet) – discussed in the FREE TEMPLATE chapter. Incredible modification capabilities with this website if you are going to use a CSS template.

Vertical Lists, Horizontal Lists, Experimental Lists and links to a plethora of other information.

HYPERGURL
http://www.hypergurl.com/generators/horizontalmenu.html

Horizontal Website Menu Generator – Online. Make your navigation menu online. No downloads needed. FREE menu generator, use as many times as you like. Multiple horizontal menu customizations and colors, mouse over and more.

THE SITE WIZARD
http://www.thesitewizard.com/wizards/css-menu-buttons.shtml
Creates a free, customized professional looking navigation menu bar for your website. Rollover or mouse over effects, no images needed, vertical and horizontal, fully customizable, plug and play, easy to create, FREE, no advertisements.

FREE WEBSITE TEMPLATES

There are many websites dedicated to selling website templates. Most of these also offer FREE website templates. There are 1000's of free website templates to choose from. A few of these websites are listed below.

- Freewebtemplates.com
- Freewebsitetemplates.com
- Freetemplatesonline.com
- Freesitetemplates.com
- Freecsstemplates.org
- Free-css-templates.com
- Zymic.com
- Bigbangtemplates.com
- Interspire.com/templates/
- Templateworld.com/free_templates.html
- Templatesbox.com/templates.htm

Browse these websites and download the website that targets the type or category of website you are looking to build. Most of these sites will attempt to steer you toward purchasing a website template for a nominal fee. Not necessary. We are attempting to build our website for FREE. Stick to your goal. These free website templates are just as good as those you will purchase.

DOWNLOADING A FREE TEMPLATE

- Walkthrough of how to proceed…

Let's presume we have selected the website www.interspire.com/templates/ as our FREE website template provider. We will begin modifying 'Free Template #158' as our sample template. Double click on this template and it will begin to download. Let's save the information in a folder that is readily accessible (on our desktop for example). Once we have the zip files downloaded, go ahead and open the zip files. Store those files on your desktop as well.

The folder will automatically be set up as "myfreetemplates-jd_m004". Let's click on the folder. **Double click on the jd_m004 folder**. The contents of the folder should look like this:

1. We should always take a look at the **readme text file** first. Double click. It is basically a terms and conditions agreement. Since, it is a free template – no problem.

2. Next let's double click on the HTML document. This is a final snapshot of the original sample template.

3. Next is the PSD or Photoshop File of the finished website as a picture. It is important to notice that the HTML file will be editable while the PSD file will not. INFRANVIEW is the default image viewer and is notifying us that it will be opening this file (if necessary).

4. Lastly, let's double click on the images file. This is pretty straight forward and stores all the images necessary for the INDEX.HTML file to view properly. For example, if we were to publish this index.html file by itself to our web host server, the image below is what we would see.

   o The empty boxes (with a little red x) are letting us know that the webpage cannot find the images being called on by the html document.

5. If we were to publish the index.html file alone without the images in the image file, we would see the webpage below on our site. No Images present.

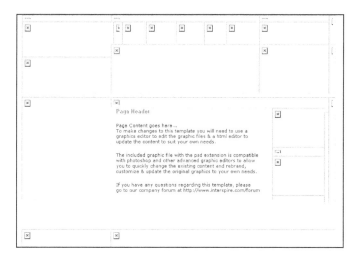

6. Let's publish the pictures in the image file into our website image file – because this is the location the html document will be looking to retrieve these images from. Now all images should be present. Once we upload the images file along with the index.html file then we have the picture

below. The webpage is loaded and can find all the pictures related to the page.

7. If you compare the picture above with the picture below, you can notice the similarities. The only constant is the text in the middle of the page. This is default text uploaded with the FREE template and is 100% editable as well.

8. Since the text is generic text and used as filler, it has no relevance or merit remaining on the page. CLEAR and UPLOAD your personalized text.

UPLOADING TO OUR WEB EDITOR

- Modifying our FREE Template

To finally begin working with our web editor, let's open our web editor and click on 'OPEN' file. Let's locate the FREE web template file we saved from the original zip download.

Once we locate the file open it and find the original INDEX file. Open the HTML file with your web editor. It will show you the completed image, as seen above. The only information you will be able to edit is the text located under the Page Header label. The rest of the website is put together through images. These images are located in the image folder. Therefore, if we want to change any of the images, we must do so directly using the image editor functions I showed you previously. DO NOT MOVE OR CHANGE THE NAME OF THE IMAGE. The INDEX.HTML file will look for these files by name and folder. If the configuration is wrong then you will get an empty box with a small x in it.

- Modifying an Image

Open your FREE download of Vicman or other image editor. Click on open file. Find your **myfreetemplates-jd_m004** file on your desktop. Double click on it until you find your **images** folder. Open up the **x3a_05** (logo) file. Use the eyedropper function to lock the background color. Now use a paintbrush and paint over the name "Your Company". All that should be left is the orange circle logo.

Now using the T or text function, type in your text -- company name. That's it. The final product will look like this in the INDEX.HTML as below.

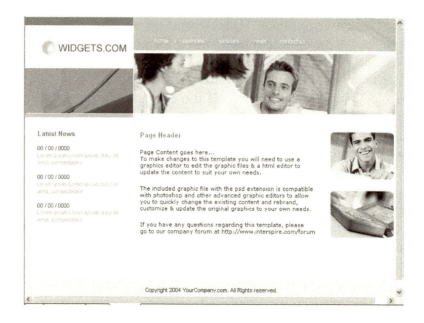

- Editing Images of a (FREE) Web Template / HTML Page

Be sure to have the correct image tag when saving a modified image. There are three primary formats to choose from:

1. PNG
2. JPG
3. GIF

We shall discuss the differences in the "What image format to use & when" chapter. For now all we need to know is that images have several formats they can be in. The three used above account for a majority of the images on the world wide web.

In our example INDEX.HTML above, the original logo file for the above web template is **x3a_05.gif** located in the image file. A simple right click of the actual logo image in our web editor (in the edit screen) gave us the file name and location to find it. Therefore, we know that the INDEX.HTML will look for this exact file and extension in the image folder once we upload to our server.

Since modifying our logo via Vicman, our ending logo file will be in the JPG format. This is a minor problem, because the image needs to be in the GIF format, as seen in the previous paragraph. Our FREE version of Vicman does not produce / modify images in the GIF format (unsure why) perhaps due to its FREE nature – pointing us to purchase the full featured model which costs money.

The easy way to go around this obstacle is to simply open the image file with photoscape and re-save it as a GIF file. Keeping the original name.

Another method, is to assign a new image (name and image format) to the area. It is crucial that the size of the image be exactly the same, or it may throw off the entire web template. Since our modified image is identical to the originals, this is not an issue.

Previous Image
x3a_05.gif

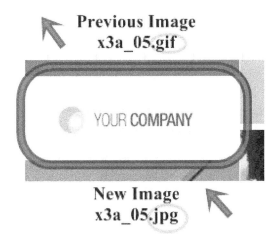

New Image
x3a_05.jpg

In your web editor, highlight the area by right clicking. Click on Image Properties. It is here that we may have the new image format into the INDEX.HTML file. In the Image Path, type in our new logo file and ending tag. **Images/x3a_05.jpg.**

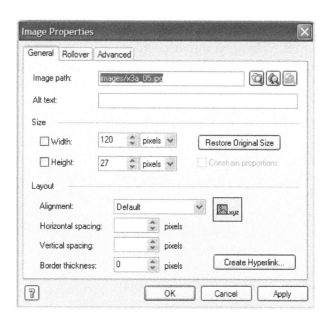

The end result will be the new company logo (which we created) show in the INDEX.HTML as seen above. Now, the INDEX.HTML document will search for our x3a_05.jpg file instead of the default x3a_05.gif file for our logo. You may change any and all of the other images in this way as well. **It is crucial to note that altering the diameters (width & height) of the images may throw off the balance of the entire website template.** Be sure to also upload the new image(s) to the web server. It is a good idea to erase or delete the pre-existing file's as well.

FREE CSS TEMPLATES

Invented in 1997, Cascading Style Sheets (CSS) are just now starting to be widely used among web developers. These style sheets are a very powerful tool for the Website developer as they give you more control and consistency with the look and feel of your web pages.

- SAVING TIME AND A LOT OF WORK

Style sheets are basically a single sheet of commands, stored separately on the web host server, which control the entire look and feel of all web pages within a website.

CSS is a breakthrough in Web design because it allows the web developers complete control over the style and layout of multiple web pages all at the same time. Let's imagine we are working on a website that consists of over 100 separate pages. We decide, before publishing to the internet, that the font size is too small for people to view comfortably. Instead of opening every page manually and fixing the problem individually, which would probably take hours. We can simply, open the Style Sheet and adjust the font size on a global scale, which will fix the entire site in seconds.

- CSS DOWNLOAD & WALKTHROUGH

Let's begin by logging onto www.freecsstemplates.org. The name of the template we will be working with is "long beach". Download the ZIP file and open. The files should look like this:

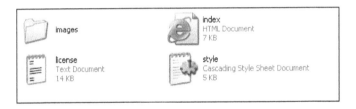

As always, let's open the license text document first. In so many words, this text document states that the "long beach" template is free and that it is ok to modify and publish.

The INDEX.HTML file is the file we will upload to our web editor and will be our beginning template for website construction. The Cascading Style Sheet Document is a vital part of the INDEX.HTML file. The CSS document gives direction on how to open the INDEX.HTML file to the web browser

Remember that when working with CSS templates, that it is crucial the CSS file be present at all times in conjunction with the webpage. Without the CSS file, the html document will fail to open properly.

When uploading our website to the web host server, we also need to upload the CSS file. Any modifications to the CSS offline, must also be saved and uploaded to the website online, to take effect. The image(s) below are examples of a website with and without a CSS attached.

INDEX.HTML file with no CSS (shown above)

INDEX.HTML file with CSS attached

- The image file contains only one picture / image. The header or long beach image.

The advantages of using CSS templates are pretty straight forward. The simple HTML format of these templates make for smaller file sizes to upload. To speed up your website additionally, it is critical that we place these CSS at the beginning of the document in between the opening and closing <head><\head> properties.

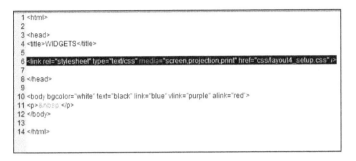

```
1 <html>
2
3 <head>
4 <title>WIDGETS</title>
5
6 <link rel="stylesheet" type="text/css" media="screen,projection,print" href="css/layout4_setup.css" />
7
8 </head>
9
10 <body bgcolor="white" text="black" link="blue" vlink="purple" alink="red">
11 <p>  </p>
12 </body>
13
14 </html>
```

This will enable the web browser to load faster. We want the browser to display whatever content it has as soon as possible. This is especially important for pages with a lot of content and for users on slower Internet connections. The browser loads the page progressively:

- The Header
- The Navigation Bar
- The Logo
- The rest of the document

All serve as visual feedback for the user who is waiting for the page to open. This improves the overall user experience.

The problem with putting style sheets near the bottom of the document is that it prohibits progressive rendering in many browsers, including Internet Explorer. These browsers block rendering to avoid having to redraw elements of the page if their styles change. Thus, user is stuck viewing a blank white page.

Modifying CSS Content

Let's load our FREE CSS template or INDEX.HTML of "long beach" into our web editor. Cycle through the different looks

067

available (e.g. EDIT, HTML & PREVIEW screens). They all look very different from one another. Modifying this template is done through the EDIT or HTML only.

As stated earlier, we will find our CSS between the opening <HEAD> and closing </HEAD> tags. Let's change the "HEADER" or title of our webpage. Located on line 25 of our HTML.

Replace "<h1><a href="#">Long Beach </a></h1>"

With "<h1><a href="#">WIDGETS</a></h1>.

Let's go ahead and view a PREVIEW of our change. Should look like the image below.

It's that simple. Remember to always keep an original of your CSS TEMPLATE somewhere safe for backup. It is also vital to constantly backup your work, as learning to work with CSS templates (and any web document format) will teach.

Removing the "design by free css templates" text is just as easy. Located one line below, on line 26, of the HTML:

<p> design by <a href="http://www.freecsstemplates.org/">Free CSS templates</a></p>

Now that we found the text we wish to remove, let's do so. Remember the href tag is setting up a hyperlink. You may have this point back to our website WIDGETS.COM.

<p> our products <a href="http://www.widgets.com/">are the best</a></p>

Modifying the rest of the INDEX.HTML file is done in the same way. Browse the HTML of the INDEX page until you arrive at the section you want to modify. *All information on the default INDEX page may be changed.*

The easiest way to identify areas when looking at HTML is by using the **EDIT & HTML** view in your web editor.

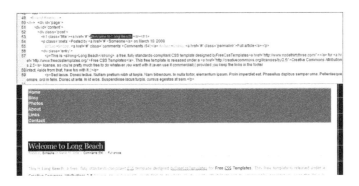

The split screen allows the user to view the EDIT screen and the HTML interface at the same time. I highly recommend this option for beginning webmasters who are learning HTML for the first time. After a little practice and patience, HTML will become a second language and is fairly simple.

Changing The Default Navigation Bar -Walkthrough

- The Navigation Bar (Grey Bar) Names & Links Associated With
  - Line 42 of the HTML
  - Be sure to change the href (#) with your link page url.
  - The default text -- <li><a href="#">Home</a></li>
  - The changed text -- <li><a href="http://www.widgets.com">Home</a></li>
  - The blue highlighted areas are editable
  - Be sure to erase the (#)

By following these easy steps, it is possible to have a professional looking website with very little work for FREE. Simply, erase and input your desired text and information in the fields you wish and save. Upload to your website. That's it.

HYPERLINKS

Hyperlinks or Links (as they are commonly known) are composed of two ends. There are anchors and a direction. The anchors are the beginning points and point to a destination URL. A link from one domain to another is said to be an outbound link from its source anchor and inbound to its target.

Web browsers display hyperlinks in some obvious ways, e.g. in a different color, font or style. Normally, links are displayed in underlined blue text.

Whether you have chosen simple text or buttons in your menu, we must assign a navigation link to them or hyperlink. A **hyperlink** is a reference or navigation element in a document to another section of the same document or to another document that may be on or part of a (different) domain. Hyperlinks are very easy to set up. If the item is simple text, then we need to highlight that word or words and right click the mouse. Click on the hyperlink button. Insert the destination hyperlink. Click OK.

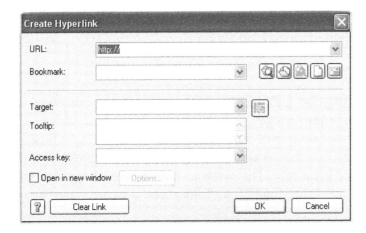

Always insert the **'HTTP://www'** at the beginning of every link. When assigning a hyperlink to a button, the procedure is the same.

An example of a hyperlink in HTML language :

<a href="*URL*" title="*link title*" target="*link target*" class="*link class*">*link label*</a>

HREF is an abbreviation for "Hypertext REFerence"

An actual hyperlink in HTML language pointing to our WIDGETS.COM webpage may be listed as:
<a href="http://www.widgets.com">WIDGETS</a>

BOOKMARKS

A bookmark is a tag that identifies a location, within a document, that is to serve as the destination of a hyperlink. Stated plainly, a bookmark will allow the visitor of a webpage to go directly to that subject.

For example, if a document has a bookmark on its webpage named "FOOTBALL STATS. Thus allowing the user to jump to that section by clicking the text or button. The web browser will jump to that location on the page, scrolling the document down (or up) if necessary. It acts as a shortcut within a website to take the viewer directly to what they are searching for.

A hyperlink on another document can refer to the bookmark by appending the bookmark name to the URL. For example, http://www.example.com/index.html#football_stats. When a user clicks the link, the browser will open the document and jump to the bookmark location. The website domain, page and bookmark are given as a map for the link to follow and open.

Bookmarks are especially useful in long documents. For example, if you have a page that contains a long list of terms and definitions, you could put a unique bookmark on each term, and then use the bookmarks to link to individual terms from other documents, or from a term index and the top of the page. It is also common to insert a bookmark at the top of a long page, and then insert links to the top bookmark periodically throughout the page. This saves users the trouble of scrolling back to the top manually.

To create a bookmark

1. The bookmark feature is created by having a beginning link and an ending point. Let's begin the bookmark process by selecting some content on the line where you want the bookmark (jump point to end up), or just place the bookmark. You may also place the bookmark anywhere on that line.
2. In the example listed below, the bookmark is placed on the highlighted text or Section_3.
3. On the Insert menu, click Bookmark; or press Ctrl + G.
4. In the Bookmark name box, type the desired name for the bookmark. If you selected text in step 1, the text will automatically appear in the box; you can edit it or replace it as you wish.
5. Click Add or press Enter, and then click Close or press Enter again.

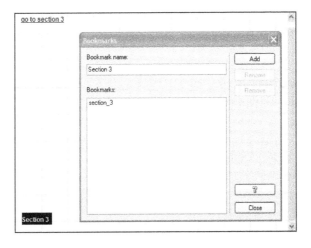

6. The next step in completing our bookmark is establishing our starting point. At the beginning of the page, or wherever you would like your starting jump point to originate, highlight text or bookmark.

7. As seen in the next example, we have highlighted the text 'go to section 3'. Now let's create a hyperlink. The hyperlink URL as shown below is '#section_3'. Click OK and were done.

8. We have just created a successful bookmark from the 'go to section 3' text (or button if desired – same procedure) to the 'Section 3' ending point.

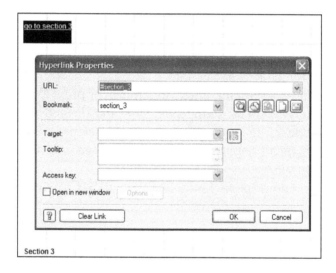

Renaming and removing bookmarks
To rename a bookmark

1. Right-click the bookmark icon or the underlined content where the desired bookmark is, and then click Modify Bookmark. (Or just double-click the bookmark icon.)
2. In the Bookmark name box, edit the bookmark name as desired and press Enter.

To delete a bookmark

1. Right-click the bookmark icon or the underlined content where the desired bookmark is, and then click Modify Bookmark. (Or just double-click the bookmark icon.)
2. Click Remove.

You can rename or delete several bookmarks at once while the Bookmarks dialog box is open. Just select each bookmark you want to rename or remove in the Bookmarks list, and then rename or remove it.

Using bookmarks in hyperlinks (jumping to another page and section)

To refer to a bookmark in the URL of a hyperlink, just append the "#" character, followed by the bookmark name, at the end of the URL. For example, to link to the bookmark named "section_8" in the document "regulations.html", you would use the URL **regulations.html#section_8**.

If you want to link to a bookmark in the same document as the link itself, just use "#" followed by the bookmark name as the URL. For example, **#section_8**.

When you create a hyperlink using the Create Hyperlink dialog box, if you enter a path to a local document in the URL box, clicking the triangle on the Bookmark box will drop down a list of all the bookmarks that are in that document. You can just select a bookmark in the list instead of typing it in.

Setting a link's target window or frame

Normally, when you click a link in a browser, the destination of that link (if it is something that can be displayed in a browser) opens in the same window or frame that displayed the document containing the link, replacing the original document. However, you can make the destination of a link open in a different window or frame from the one displaying the current document. You do this by specifying the link's target.

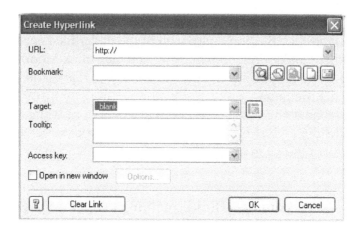

A link's target can be the name of a window, the name of a frame, or one of these special keywords:

- **_blank**: The link will be opened in a new, unnamed window.
- **_parent**: The link will be opened in the current frame's "parent", replacing the current frameset. The parent is usually the browser window, but if the current frameset is being displayed inside one frame of another frameset, then the parent is the containing frame in the higher-level frameset.
- **_self**: The link will be opened in the current frame or window.
- **_top**: The link will be opened in the current window. If the window is divided into frames, the link's destination will replace the frames.

A window's name is not the same as its title, the words that appear in its title bar. If a window has a name, it is not visible to users, but the browser remembers it as long as the window is open. To create a browser window with a certain name, set the target of a hyperlink to the desired name. If you want the named window to be initially empty, set the link's URL to "about: blank".

In general, there is no reason to set the target of a single hyperlink to a named window. However, if you have several hyperlinks that you would like to open in a separate window from the current document, but you don't want a new window to be opened for each link, you can set all of the links' targets to one window name. When the first link in the group is clicked, the browser will create a new window and open the link in it. Then, when other links in the group are clicked, they will open in the same window.

This is the procedure that give's you more control in how your visitor's will view your webpage's and content. The webmaster has total control in how the content or information will be viewed. Take this into consideration in setting up a nice display for your visitors when viewing your webpage's.

To set a link's target

1. Double-click the link to open the Hyperlink Properties dialog box.
2. In the Target box, type the desired frame or window name, or click the triangle and select one of the keywords or frame names (if a frameset is open). If a frameset is currently open.

You can also set a link's target using the Target box on the Hyperlink Toolbar. Type a window or frame name in the box or click the triangle and select one of the keywords or frame names.

You may go back at any time and modify any or ALL of your link's targets at any time.

FAVICON

Favicon is short for favorite's icon. Also known as a **website icon**, **shortcut icon**, **url icon**, or **bookmark icon** is an icon associated with a particular website or webpage. A web designer can create such an icon and install it into a website (or webpage) by several means, and most graphical web browsers will then make use of it. Browsers that provide favicon support typically display a page's favicon in the browser's URL bar and next to the page's name in a list of bookmarks. Browsers that support a tabbed document interface typically show a page's favicon next to the page's title.

Favicon's add to a website's identity. By simply seeing the website icon or logo, a visitor can easy relate to the website homepage and identify what the site is.

Creating a Favicon is very simple and installing it is very easy. By now, you are pretty far along in creating your website. You may even have a logo created or saved. If not, we will need to download a Favicon or create one now.

There are a lot of FREE Favicon website's out there. Some site's also create or generate favicon's for a fee. But we already know that. Some FREE example favicon's:

Mobilephone2

Mobilephone3

Money

ICONARCHIVE.COM
The Icon Archive is a categorized collection of high quality desktop & web icon sets. Over 23,800 icons in 849 sets from 203 icon authors. Icons can be used for Windows (XP, Vista, etc.), Macintosh (OSX, OS) and Linux (as PNG Files).

FREEFAVICON.COM is a great site for creating and downloading generic favicons. Simply upload your image into there form and that's it. They will generate your Favicon in ICO form.

- Keep the graphic simple. You don't have a lot of space to work with, so focus on the most important parts. Complex logos and graphics don't work well.

- Start with a square image. The favicon will be scaled to be square. If you start with a rectangle it will be distorted.

ADSEN FAVICON 1.2 is a simple favicon freeware creator that lets people make a favicon ico for their website, which shows up in IE's favorites. It is downloadable, which means you can experiment and create as many favicon's as you wish.

It can use either bmp or jpg files, and will convert them to ico format using the size and color quality you choose. Not only can you create favicons, but it can also be used for creating icons for programs. Adsen FavIcon comes with notes on what settings to use for making favicons and how to install them.

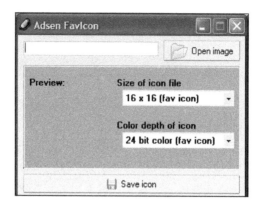

Download FREE program:
http://adsen-favicon.adsen-software.qarchive.org.

What is an ico file?

An ico file is actually a repository of bitmap like images. They are used because in some locations a 16x16 pixel image is desired, and sometimes a 32x32 image may be needed. Sometimes a 16 color image is desired, and sometimes a 256 color icon is desired. This repository is scanned for the image size/color count appropriate for the location and the computer's color capability. If the image is not ideal, it may be compressed, expanded, and/or colors may be modified producing unexpected results.

FAVICON SETUP – IMPORTANT INFORMATION

1. The favorite icon must be named **FAVICON.ICO**
2. Ideally, size 16 x 16 and 24 bit color is best
3. Insert the line below into your HTML between the <head> and </head> tags

    <link rel="shortcut icon" href="favicon.ico">

4. The Favicon must be uploaded to the same folder that contains the webpage.
5. The Favicon may take up to a week to show on your web browser. Be patient.

WEBSITE IMAGES & PICTURES

When to use them

In working with images on our website, we should understand the differences in image formats available and their corresponding quality attributes. There are many commonly used image file formats. Part of the reason for the plethora of file types is the need for *compression*.

Image files can be quite large, and larger file types mean more disk usage and slower downloads. Compression is a term used to describe ways of cutting the size of the file.

Another reason for the many file types is that images differ in the number of colors they contain. If an image has few colors, a file type can be designed to exploit this as a way of reducing file size.

Number of colors

Images start with differing numbers of colors in them. The simplest images may contain only two colors, such as black and white, and will need only 1 bit to represent each pixel. Many early PC video cards would support only 16 fixed colors. Later cards would display 256 simultaneously, any of which could be chosen from a pool of 2^{24}, or 16 million colors. New cards devote 24 bits to each pixel, and are therefore capable of displaying 2^{24}, or 16 million colors without restriction. A few display even more. Since the eye has trouble distinguishing between similar colors, 24 bit or 16 million colors is often called TrueColor.

Lossy vs. Lossless compression

A lossless compression algorithm discards no information. It looks for more efficient ways to represent an image, while making no compromises in accuracy. In contrast, lossy algorithms accept some degradation in the image in order to achieve smaller file size.

A lossless algorithm might, for example, look for a recurring pattern in the file, and replace each occurrence with a short abbreviation, thereby cutting the file size. In contrast, a lossy algorithm might store color information at a lower resolution than the image itself, since the eye is not so sensitive to changes in color of a small distance.

The GIF image format

GIF stands for *Graphics Interchange Format*. Developed by CompuServe to show images online in 1987 for 8 bit video boards. Today, it is probably the most common image format used on the Web. GIFs have the advantage of usually being very small in size, which makes them fast-loading. Unlike JPEGs, GIFs use *lossless* compression, which means they make the file size small without losing or blurring any of the image itself.

GIFs also support *transparency*, which means that they can sit on top of a background image on your web page without having ugly rectangles around them.

Another cool thing that GIFs can do is animation. You can make an animated GIF by drawing each frame of the animation in a graphics package that supports the animated GIF format, then export the animation to a single GIF file. When you include this file in your Web page (with the img tag), your animation will be displayed on the page!

The major disadvantage of GIFs is that they only support up to 256 colours (this is known as *8-bit colour* and is a type of *indexed colour* image). This means they're not good for photographs, or any other image that contains lots of different colours. However, GIF's are still an excellent format for graphics on the world wide web today for images like logos or dialog boxes that only use a few colors. Being limited to 256 colors is not important for a 3 color logo afterall.

Making Fast-Loading GIFs

It's worthwhile making your GIF file sizes as small as possible, so that your Web pages load quickly. People will get very bored otherwise, and probably go to another website!

Most graphics programs let you control various settings when making a GIF image, such as palette size (number of colours in the image) and dithering. Generally, speaking, use the smallest palette size you can. Usually 32 colour palette produce acceptable results, although for low-colour images you can often get away with 16. Images with lots of colours will of course need a bigger palette - say, 128, or even 256 colours.

8-colour GIF (1292 bytes)   64-colour GIF (2940 bytes)

The JPEG Image Format

JPEG stands for *Joint Photographic Experts Group*, a bunch of individuals who invented this format to display full-colour photographic images in a portable format with a small file size. Like GIF images, they are also very common on the Web. Their main advantage over GIFs is that they can display true-colour images (up to 16 million colours), which makes them much better for images such as photographs and illustrations with large numbers of colours.

The main disadvantage of the JPEG format is that it is *lossy*. This means that you lose some of the detail of your image when you convert it to JPEG format. Boundaries between blocks of colour may appear more blurry, and areas with lots of detail will lose their sharpness. On the other hand, JPEGs do preserve all of the colour information in the image, which of course is great for high-colour images such as photographs.

Even worse, more quality is lost every time the JPG file is compressed and saved again, so ever editing and saving a JPG image again is a questionable decision. You should instead just discard the old JPG file and start over from your archived lossless TIF master, saving that change as the new JPG copy you need. JPG compression can be selected to be better quality in a larger file, or to be lesser quality in a smaller file. When you save a JPG file, your FILE - SAVE AS dialog box should have an option for the degree of file compression.

JPEGs also can't do transparency or animation - in these instances, you will have to use the GIF format (or PNG format for transparency).

Making Fast-Loading JPEGs

As with GIFs, it pays to make your JPEG's as small as possible (in terms of bytes), so that your websites will load quickly. The main control over file size with JPEGs is called *quality*, and usually varies from 0 to 100%, where 0% is low quality (but smallest file size), and 100% is highest quality (but largest file size). 0% quality JPEGs usually look noticeably blurred when compared to the original. 100% quality JPEGs are often indistinguishable from the original:

Low-quality JPEG (4089 bytes)

High-quality JPEG (17465 bytes)

The PNG Image Format

PNG is a relatively new invention compared to GIF or JPEG, although it's been around for a while now. (Sadly some browsers such as IE6 still don't support them fully.) It stands for *Portable Network Graphics*. It was designed to be an alternative to the GIF file format, but without the licensing issues that were involved in the GIF compression method at the time.

There are two types of PNG: *PNG-8* format, which holds 8 bits of colour information (comparable to GIF), and *PNG-24* format, which holds 24 bits of colour (comparable to JPEG).

PNG-8 often compresses images even better than GIF, resulting in smaller file sizes. On the other hand, PNG-24 is often less effective than JPEGs at compressing true-colour images such as photos, resulting in larger file sizes than the equivalent quality JPEGs. However, unlike JPEG, PNG-24 is lossless, meaning that all of the original image's information is preserved.

PNG also supports transparency like GIF, but can have varying degrees of transparency for each pixel, whereas GIFs can only have transparency turned on or off for each pixel. This means that whereas transparent GIFs often have jagged edges when placed on complex or ill-matching backgrounds, transparent PNGs will have nice smooth edges.

Note that unlike GIF, PNG-8 does not support animation. One important point about PNG: Earlier browsers don't recognize them. If you want to ensure your website is viewable by early browsers, use GIF's or JPEGs instead.

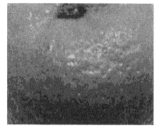 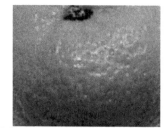

16-colour PNG-8 (6481 bytes)   Full-colour PNG-24 (34377 bytes)

PNG's compression is among the best that can be had without losing image information.

Summary of image formats

This table summarizes the key differences between the GIF, JPEG and PNG image formats.

GIF	JPEG	PNG-8	PNG-24
Better for clipart and drawn graphics with few colours, or large blocks of colour	Better for photographs with lots of colours or fine colour detail	Better for clipart and drawn graphics with few colours, or large blocks of colour	Better for photographs with lots of colours or fine colour detail
Can only have up to 256 colours	Can have up to 16 million colours	Can only have up to 256 colours	Can have up to 16 million colours
Images are "lossless" - they contain the same amount of information as the original (but with only 256 colours)	Images are "lossy" - they contain less information than the original	Images are "lossless" - they contain the same amount of information as the original (but with only 256 colours)	Images are "lossless" - they contain the same amount of information as the original
Can be animated	Cannot be animated	Cannot be animated	Cannot be animated
Can have transparent areas	Cannot have transparent areas	Can have transparent areas	Can have transparent areas

On the whole, GIFs are better for the Web, as Web graphics tend to be small, have a small amount of colours, and sometimes need fancy stuff like animation or transparency. However, JPEGs are really handy when you have a very complex or large image (such as a photo), and/or you want a full colour image. PNG-8 can often produce smaller file sizes than GIF, and both types of PNG are lossless.

Remember, keeping your webpage file size low is what we are striving for. The smaller these file sizes are, the faster the upload times are. The smaller the image files are the better the code-to-text (discussed later) ratio will be, which in turn shall boost our PageRank (Google's ranking system for websites).

Top FREE Image Editors - Working with images

As mentioned in the 'Initial Web Design' chapter, the best image editors are:

- **PHOTOSCAPE** – Download from Cnet
- **VICMAN'S PHOTO EDITOR** – Download from www.vicman.net
- **INFRANVIEW 4.2** (or better version) – Download from Cnet
- **COOLTEXT.COM** – Free Logo Generator & More

Rip images from the world wide web for use in our website

Now that we understand the basic differences in a JPG, GIF and PNG image formats. Let's continue by retrieving or ripping a few FREE files from the web and inputting them into our website.

Let's log onto Google's Image Search -- http://www.images.google.com

Let's work with "COMPANY LOGOS". Remember to place the mouse upon the image and right click. "SAVE IMAGE AS", place in your folder and save.

A few notable logos we have ripped or downloaded are:

These images are highly recognizable and would not be good examples of logo templates to alter as they are trademarked. However, they are easily downloaded. Let's find some FREE logo templates that we CAN modify for use in our website.

Our FREE logo template will be downloaded from:
http://www.templatesbox.com/free-logo-templates/index.htm

We will be working with *Logo Template #FL054*

Open your copy of PHOTOSCAPE and continue on to the 'editor' screen. Find the logo056.jpg file and select. Next, click on the "Object" tab at the bottom of your editor.

Click on the square option with the "white" FILL checked. Surround the default text in the logo until only the circular image remains.

Now you have a blank slate and can add any name or information you want. By clicking on the "T" in the OBJECT tab, you can add some text. You can change color and size of text separately.

Modifying images and picture's is a very simple procedure. In this manner, we can take generic images and make them our own. When saving, the image editor will ask you for the format you will like to save your image to: JPG, GIF or PNG.

For those who are just starting out, let's save the image to all three image formats. You will have three exact images, differing only in the format they have been saved to. Now look at the differences in quality versus the file size. We want the best of both worlds. Great visual image and low file size. Once you become more comfortable with which format is best for your image, save only once.

RSS FEEDS

Typically, RSS (Really Simple Syndication) feeds are a group of Web feed formats used to publish frequently updated works – such as blog entries, news headlines, audio and video. Typical RSS logos are:

RSS feeds are commonly used in today's world wide web. RSS feeds allow us, the webmaster, the means and opportunity to setup our websites with FREE fresh content on a daily basis. RSS feeds are also highly customizable – we receive information and updates in a format we choose. *Depending on the feed we are using, our website will update on its own without any further action on our parts, supplying our readers constantly with new and fresh information.*

There are thousands of FREE feeds on the internet. What type of feed will augment our website and be of valuable content to our viewers. Types of Feeds available:

☐ News RSS feeds
☐ Politics RSS feeds
☐ Sports RSS feeds
☐ Lifestyle RSS feeds
☐ Entertainment RSS feeds
☐ Multimedia RSS feeds

☐ Columnists RSS feeds
☐ Blog RSS feeds
☐ Cars RSS feeds
☐ Homes RSS feeds
☐ Jobs RSS feeds

Walkthrough – Setting up an RSS feed on our site

1. Finding a RSS feed to work with.

Initially, let's find a RSS feed to work with. This is done by clicking onto a popular website, such as YAHOO.COM, WSJ.COM (Wall Street Journal), CNNFN.com, etc. Locate the RSS feeds button / logo, usually found on the bottom of the webpage.

Let's work with cnnfn.com. Log onto their site and go to the bottom of the page. Double click on the RSS text. This will take us to a page with multiple RSS feeds. Find the Feed you would like to work with.

Let's work with the ALL STORIES feed at the top.

Click on the XML feed. That is the one we will use to customize this feed into our website. The other buttons: YAHOO, GOOGLE, MY AOL & NETVIBES are different RSS readers used to view these feeds. We will not need them.

The XML page should look like the image above. This page will ask you to "SUBSCRIBE NOW" to different readers and "learn more" about this and that. The important information is in the **ADDRESS BAR** at the top.

OUR RSS FEED   http://money.cnn.com/services/rss/

The "Current Feed Content" is what is currently on the RSS feed. Also, it will have the POSTED dates. Scroll down through a few articles and pay attention to these dates. We want to have much NEW information as possible on our website daily. Look for as many posts with today's date as possible. Certain RSS feeds may post only one article a week or month. Those are not the one's we are looking for.

2. **Customizing our RSS feed and preparing it for website insertion.**

Using the website RSS-INFO.com (a free RSS feed converter website), connect to their RSSINCLUDE page [http://www.rss-info.com/en_rssinclude-simple.html]. You will see the image below.

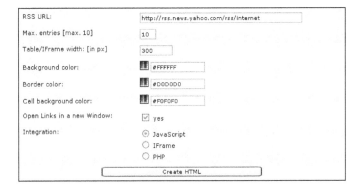

- **RSS URL :**   Insert 'Our RSS Feed'
- **MAX ENTRIES:**   The feed we setup in our website may have anywhere from 1 to 10 articles update a day. This is important when we are attempting to balance our website. For example, we do not want the left column of our website going on and on, when the content in the middle and right

columns have stopped. In this way, we can go back and adjust our 10 articles a day to 4 articles. That will shorten the feed and balance our site visually.

- **TABLE WIDTH:** Table width is pretty straight forward. If your feed is too wide or narrow, this is where you can modify that info.
- **BACKGROUND COLOR:** Most background color is #FFFFFF (white). However, if your background color is another color and you aren't sure of its composure, there is a simple trick to find out.

  Open your HTML editor. Open your INDEX.HTML file or the webpage where the feed will be placed. In your EDIT or PREVIEW view of this page, locate where you are planning to place the feed. The color you are trying to mimic should be present at that location.
  At the top of the screen in the EDIT view is the FONT Button. Click on the eyedropper function. Now go to that location on your website you are attempting to find the color for. That's it. Plug this six digit code into the Background Color Box above. If the color is a shading or blend that is not constant, you may need to play with this option in your RSSinclude to best match your background for your RSS Feed.

- **BORDER COLOR:** Your RSS feed will be in the form of a box. Whether you want it to blend into your website or stand out is your option. This feature will allow you to put a thin line around your feed box so that it will stand out more.
- **CELL BACKGROUND COLOR:** Primary background for your Feed Boxes
- **OPEN LINKS IN A NEW WINDOW:** We would like our visitors / viewers to remain on our website for as long as possible, therefore, if they click on any of these RSS links – we would choose to have that link open in a new window.
- **INTEGRATION: JAVASCRIPT / IFRAME / PHP**
  JAVASCRIPT: Is a scripting language which is most often used for web development and is easier for non-programmers to work with.

IFRAME: Is an HTML element which serves as a window. It allows for the embedding of a HTML document inside another HTML document.

PHP: Is also a scripting language. These PHP scripts are usually designed for dynamic web pages. In layman's terms: allows for small scripting engines to execute functions decided by either the programmer (client-side) or the visitors web browser (server-side) decided by their input, environmental conditions (such as the time of day), or other variables that usually provide interactive web sites, that interface to databases or other data stores.

Using JavaScript our end result is :

To integrate this feed into your website, please copy the following HTML code into your page:

```
<script language="javascript" src="http://www.rss-
info.com/rss2.php?integration=js&windowopen=1&rss=http%3A%2F%
2Frss.cnn.com%2Frss%
2Fmoney_latest.rss&number=3&width=350&ifbgcol=eeeeee&bordercol=D
0D0D0&textbgcol=f7f7f7&rssbgcol=f7f7f7&showrsstitle=1&showtext=1
```

Highlight and copy this script in its entirety. Place in your HTML Editor on the web page you desire. Save and Upload to your web host server. You should see the following image:

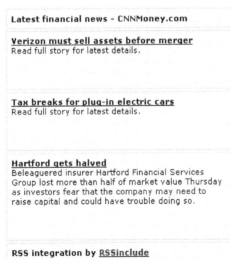

Latest financial news - CNNMoney.com

Verizon must sell assets before merger
Read full story for latest details.

Tax breaks for plug-in electric cars
Read full story for latest details.

Hartford gets halved
Beleaguered insurer Hartford Financial Services Group lost more than half of market value Thursday as investors fear that the company may need to raise capital and could have trouble doing so.

RSS integration by RSSinclude

The RSS integration tag at the bottom is a simple one way link which cannot be removed. RSS-INFO.com serves over 250,000 feeds a day. The tag at the bottom of our FEED is a minimal price to pay for using the great FREE converter (RSSinclude).

CREATING A SITEMAP FILE AND WHY??

CREATING A SITEMAP FILE AND WHY??

SITEMAP FILE

A sitemap is a way of organizing a website, identifying the URLs and the data under each section. Think of your Sitemap as a "table of contents" for search engines like Google and Yahoo to find information buried within your website. A sitemap is the entire list of pages you are planning on building or have up and running for your website. As previously stated, your website may consist of only one page or thousands.

Your website's layout and depth is 100% dependent on your passion and creativity. It's basically up to you (and the type of web host server you have opted to use) to build and list these pages. The FREE web hosts are good (considering you haven't spent a dime and have a website up and running), however, the one I recommended with IXWEBHOSTING.COM has tons and tons of options and bandwidth the other FREE hosts do not provide.

CREATE YOUR SITEMAP

A Sitemap or site index is a general top-down view of the overall site contents. It is basically a list of every page associated with your website. Sitemaps are an easy way for webmasters to inform search engines about pages on their sites that are available for crawling.

In its simplest form, a Sitemap is an XML file that lists URLs for a site along with additional metadata about each URL (when it was last updated, how often it usually changes, and how important it is, relative to other URLs in the site) so that search engines can more intelligently crawl the site.

Web crawlers usually discover pages from links within the site and from other sites. Sitemaps supplement this data to allow crawlers that support Sitemaps to pick up all URLs in the Sitemap and learn about those URLs using the associated metadata. Using the Sitemap protocol does not guarantee that web pages are included in search engines, but provides hints for web crawlers to do a better job of crawling your site.

To explain visually, a sitemap is a roadmap of a website. It tells the Search Engine's where to look for new and old webpage's that may be buried deeper than the SE would typically look.

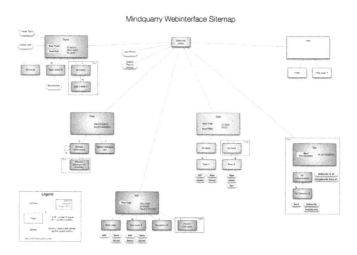

Mindquarry Webinterface Sitemap

Types of Sitemaps

- **XML Sitemaps** - The Sitemap Protocol format consists of XML tags. The file itself must be UTF-8 encoded.

```
<?xml version='1.0' encoding='UTF-8'?>
<urlset xmlns="http://www.sitemaps.org/schemas/sitemap/0.9"
        xmlns:xsi="http://www.w3.org/2001/XMLSchema-instance"
        xsi:schemaLocation="http://www.sitemaps.org/schemas/sitemap/0.9
                            http://www.sitemaps.org/schemas/sitemap/0.9/sitemap.xsd">
    <url>
        <loc>http://w3c-at.de</loc>
        <lastmod>2006-11-18</lastmod>
        <changefreq>daily</changefreq>
        <priority>0.8</priority>
    </url>
</urlset>
```

Free Online Resource → www.xml-sitemaps.com

- **RSS / ATOM Feed** - Google accepts RSS (Real Simple Syndication) 2.0 and Atom 1.0 feeds. If you have a blog with an RSS or Atom feed, you submit the feed's URL as a Sitemap. Most blog software creates your feed for you.

- **Sitemap based on Sitemap Protocol**

```
To create a Sitemap based on the Sitemap protocol:
1. Create a text file and save it with a .xml extension.
2. Add the following to the top of the file:

   <?xml version="1.0" encoding="UTF-8"?>

    <urlset xmlns="http://www.sitemaps.org/schemas/sitemap/0.9">

3. Add the following to the bottom of the file:

   </urlset>

4. Create an entry for each URL. The <loc> tag is required; the others are optional.

   <url>
       <loc>http://www.example.com/</loc>
       <lastmod>2005-01-01</lastmod>
       <changefreq>monthly</changefreq>
       <priority>0.8</priority>
   </url>
```

- **Video Sitemaps** - A Video Sitemap is simply a structured feed (in the Media RSS format with Google extensions) that contains URLs for one or more video files that you would like Google to index. Associated with each URL is descriptive information - such as a video's title, summary, transcript, etc - that makes it easier for users to find a particular piece of content.
- **Mobile Sitemaps** - A Mobile Sitemap uses the Sitemap protocol, along with a specific tag and an additional namespace requirement. Note that the Mobile Sitemap format is changing. We recommend that you update your Mobile Sitemaps to the format below as soon as you can.

```
<?xml version="1.0" encoding="UTF-8" ?>
 <urlset xmlns="http://www.sitemaps.org/schemas/sitemap/0.9"
  xmlns:mobile="http://www.google.com/schemas/sitemap-mobile/1.0">
    <url>
        <loc>http://mobile.example.com/article100.html</loc>
        <mobile:mobile/>
    </url>
</urlset>
```

- **News Sitemaps** - All articles in a News Sitemap must have the same publication label. Roughly speaking, a publication label specifies the publication name and language. For instance, if a site publishes *The Example Times (English)* and

Journal Exemplaire (Français), then it would have two publication labels, one for each of these publications.

- **Code Search Sitemaps** - Google's Code Search helps users find function definitions and sample code by enabling them to search publicly accessible source code hosted on the Internet. You can tell Google about source code on your site by creating and submitting a Code Search Sitemap.

- **Sitemap based on a Text File**

Which format should I use? Good question. The easiest sitemap to generate on your own, which is generally accepted by GOOGLE & YAHOO is the *sitemap based on a text file*.

There are many FREE automatic sitemap generators out there. I encourage you attempt to work with a few of them. Your site does not have to be completed to create a sitemap of it. A list of Sitemap generator's can be found at http://xmlsitemap.com. These websites often allow users to use their software to get links back to their website. Their software will encode it's sitemap of your website with their name attached to it, as seen in the RSS section of this book.

A Sitemap should contain a list of your site's URLs - up to 50,000 of them. If you have a large site with more than 50,000 URLs, you should create multiple Sitemaps and submit a Sitemap index file .

You can provide Google with a simple text file that contains one URL per line. For example:

http://www.example.com/file1.html

http://www.example.com/file2.html

For best results, follow these guidelines:

1. You must fully specify URLs as Google attempts to crawl them exactly as provided.
2. Each text file can contain a maximum of 50,000 URLs. If you site includes more than 50,000 URLs, you can separate the list into multiple text files and add each one separately.
3. The text file must use UTF-8 encoding. You can specify this when you save the file (for instance, in Notepad, this is listed in the Encoding menu of the Save As dialog box).
4. The text file should contain no information other than the list of URLs.
5. The text file should contain no header or footer information.
6. You can name the text file anything you wish. Google recommends giving the file a .txt extension to identify it as a text file (for instance, sitemap.txt).

You should upload the text file to your server, generally to the highest-level directory you want search engines to crawl. Once you've created this file, you can submit it as a Sitemap. This process, while manual, is the simplest and is probably best if you're not familiar with scripting or managing your web server.

Walkthrough – Setting Up Your Sitemap

1. Have a list on hand of the webpage's you would like Search Engines like Google and Yahoo to index or cache.

2. Beginning the process: **Open up your notepad**. (Typically found in your accessories folder). Click on the START button. Click on ALL BUTTONS. Click on ACCESSORIES. This is where it should be.

3. You should now have a blank page open. It should say "Untitled-notepad" on the top of the page.

4. Simply begin listing your webpage's from top to bottom (homepage or index on top). Don't forget to type in the **HTTP://WWW a**t the beginning of your links.

5. For example:

http://www.yourwebsite.com/index.html

http://www.yourwebsite.com/2ndpage.html

http://www.yourwebsite.com/3rdpage.html

http://www.yourwebsite.com/4thpage.html

http://www.yourwebsite.com/5thpage.html

http://www.yourwebsite.com/lastpage.html

6. Next step, saving the file correctly.

7. Click on the FILE button (top left of page).

8. Click on SAVE AS. Should look like the image below.

9. Under the SAVE IN folder at the top. Place the text file in with the rest of your website templates or HTML's. You will need to find this file later for uploading.

10. Time to name our file. Erase the default script in the FILE NAME slot (*.txt), you will not need it. Type in name. Let's name this file SITEMAP. Theoretically, you can name it anything you would like.

11. Now under the SAVE AS TYPE, it will be a text document.

12. Finally, and the most important step of the whole process, ENCODING. The encoding must be set for **UTF-8**. The other encoding options will not work with Search Engine submittal later.

13. Upload your SITEMAP.TXT file to your website.

14. Generally, you will not have any links to this webpage. Remember, it is there for the Search Engines to access.

15. You may view this page by typing in your webpage and the sitemap extension or http://www.yourwebsite.com/sitemap.txt.

Let's submit our SITEMAP to Google for indexing

If we haven't already done so, let's create a Google Account. It is 100% free and gives us incredible webmaster tools to aid in the development and promotion of our site.

Visit → www.google.com/sitemaps

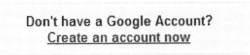

Be sure to keep your account Log In and Password somewhere readily available. You will be visiting this site often. Once logged in "ADD SITE". Enter your website.

Next you will be asked to verify your website. There are two methods of doing this.

1. Add a meta tag (or)
2. Upload and HTML file

Once you have completed adding a meta tag or uploading an HTML file log back into www.google.com/sitemaps and click on "verify". If you have done so correctly, you will see the website successfully verified message.

Next let's include your sitemap, so Google can search through every page of your site and store it. The more information you have stored the better. When someone is searching Google for an item that relates to your site or product, you will be listed. Increasing your ranking will be discussed in later chapters.

Next, click on the Sitemaps link →

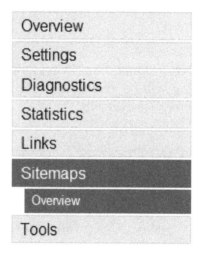

This is where you submit your sitemap location to Google. That's it. You have now successfully & officially submitted your site to Google. You can check back from time to time to see how your website is performing:

- What pages of your site have been indexed and cached

- What links you have (internal & external)

- Statistics (top searches, keyword performance, etc.)

- Diagnostics (web crawl, content analysis, etc.)

ROBOT.TXT FILE

WHY DO I NEED ONE?

A robot.txt file is a simple way to control what pages are indexed on your site and what page's you do not want recorded or cached for search. It instructs the search engine robots and web spiders to keep out of those areas.

GENERAL RULES

The simplest robots.txt file uses two rules:

> **User-agent**: the robot the following rule applies to (targeting individual bots and their accessibility to your website).

> **Disallow**: the URL you want to block from all robots.

There are a large number of FREE robot.txt generator's out there. The file is extremely simple to create and maintain manually. We should remember that those site's, although FREE to use, will generate our file and tag on a backlink from your site (as payment for using their software).

Web Robot's Database or http://www.robotstxt.org/db.html lists over 300 web robots active on the internet today. Access to their site and a list of these robots is FREE and available for use.

You can set an entry to apply to a specific bot (by listing the name) or you can set it to apply to all bots (by listing an asterisk). An entry that applies to all bots looks like this:

User-agent: *

To block the entire site, use a forward slash.
Disallow: /

To block a directory and everything in it, follow the directory name with a forward slash.
Disallow: /junk-directory/

To block a page, list the page.
Disallow: /private_file.html

To remove a specific image from Google image search, add the following:
User-agent: Googlebot-Image
Disallow: /images/dogs.jpg

To remove all images on your site from Google image search:
User-agent: Googlebot-Image
Disallow: /

To block files of a specific file type (for example, .gif), use the following:
User-agent: Googlebot
Disallow: /*.gif$

Walkthrough – Setting Up ROBOT.TXT File

1. Have a list on hand of the webpage's you would like these robot's to have access to and the one's you want to block.
2. Beginning the process: **Open up your notepad**. (Typically found in your accessories folder). Click on the START button. Click on ALL BUTTONS. Click on ACCESSORIES. This is where it should be.
3. You should now have a blank page open. It should say "Untitled-notepad" on the top of the page.
4. Now let's type in the user-agent and disallow functions and the robots and / or webpage's we want to control accessibility to and from. The example below is a simple list which allows accessibility to all webpage's by any and all robots (user-agent). The Disallow functions listed below restrict all robots from accessing these webpage's or folders on our website.
5. For example:

User-Agent: *
Disallow: /cgi-bin/
Disallow: /images/
Disallow: /reciprocal.html
Disallow: /index2.html
Disallow: /cse
Disallow: /linkdiy.php
Disallow: /linkexchanged.php
Disallow: /gotlinks.php
Disallow: /gimmielinks.html
Disallow: /linktrade.php
Disallow: /linkmachine

6. Next step, saving the file correctly.
7. Click on the FILE button (top left of page).
8. Click on SAVE AS.
9. Under the SAVE IN folder at the top. Place the text file in with the rest of your website templates or HTML's. You will need to find this file later for uploading.
10. Time to name our file. Erase the default script in the FILE NAME slot (*.txt), you will not need it. Type in name. Let's name this file ROBOT. Theoretically, you can name it anything you would like. It is important that we use **lowercase** when naming this file.
11. Now under the SAVE AS TYPE, it will be a text document.
12. Finally, and the most important step of the whole process, ENCODING. The encoding must be set for **ASCII**. The other encoding options will not work with Search Engine submittal later.
13. Upload your ROBOT.TXT file to your website. Once you've created your robots.txt file, save it to the root of your domain with the name robots.txt. This is where robots will check for your file. If it's saved elsewhere, they won't find it.
14. Generally, you will not have any links to this webpage. Remember, it is there for the Search Engines to access.
15. You may view this page by typing in your webpage and the sitemap extension or http://www.yourwebsite.com/robot.txt.

META TAGS

What are Meta tags?

META tags are part of HTML but are there for the sole use of search engine spiders. To answer the question: Are Meta tags necessary....the answer is definitely YES! These (numerous) tags contain various information that the site owner wants to deliver to these Search Engine spiders. These are used to identify the pages by both browsers and search engines. Meta tags provide keywords and descriptions on pages that for some reason may lack text. There are several Meta tags, but the most important for search engine indexing are the description and keywords tags. The description tag returns a description of the page in place of the summary the search engine would ordinarily create. The keywords tag provides keywords for the search engine to associate with your page.

Types of Meta Tags and their uses

Abstract META Tag (Suggested) - Generally the Abstract META tag is a one line sentence which gives an overview of the entire webpage.

> META Name: "Abstract"
> General Usage: <META name="Abstract" content="Abstract phrase">

Author META Tag (Optional) - The author META tag defines the name of the author of the document being read.

> META Name: "Author"
> General Usage: <META name="Author" content="Author Information">

Copyright META Tag (Optional) - The copyright META tag defines any copyright statements you wish to disclose about your webpage documents. You may wish to indicate any trademark names, patent numbers, copyright or other information which you want to publicly disclose as your intellectual property.

> META Name: "Copyright"
> General Usage: <META name="Copyright"
> content="Copyright Statement">

Description META Tags (Strongly Suggested) - Search engines that support META tags will often display the Description META tag along with your title in their results. Search engines will often capture the entire META tag of your description field, but webmasters should bear in mind that when a search engine displays the results to a user, the space is limited, usually under 20 words which you can use to grab the attention of a user. For this reason, when creating your META tags, webmasters should make the first sentence of their description field to capture the attention of a user and use the rest of the description tag to elaborate further.

> META Name: "Description"
> General Usage: <META name="Description" content="Your description">

Distribution META Tag (Optional) - The distribution META tag defines the level or degree of distribution of your webpage and how it should be classified in relation to methods of distribution on the world wide web. There are currently only three forms of distribution supported by the distribution tag: Global (indicates that your webpage is intended for mass distribution to everyone), Local (intended for local distribution of your document), and IU - Internal Use (not intended for public distribution).

> META Name: "Distribution"
> Supported Distributions: Global | Local | IU

General Usage: <META name="Distribution" content="Global">
Note: Only use one of the above

Expires META Tag (Optional) - Overview: The Expires Tag declares to search engines when the content on your website will expire. The Expires META tag defines the expiration date and time of the document being indexed. If your website is running a limited time event or there is a preset date when your document will no longer be valid, you should include the Expires tag to indicate to search engines when to delete your webpage from their database.

> META Name: "Expires"
> General Usage: <META name="Expires" content="Tue, 01 Jun 1999 19:58:02 GMT">
> Note: Requires RFC1123 date as shown above

Keyword META Tag (Strongly Suggested) - Overview: The Keywords Tag is a series of keywords that represents the content of your site. Search engines that support META tags will often use the keywords found on your pages as a means to categorize your website based on the search engines indexing algorithms (proprietary algorithms which index your website in search engine databases). Ensure you choose keywords that are relevant to your site and avoid excessive repetition as many search engines will penalize your rankings for attempting to abuse their system. Similar to the Description META Tag, search engines give priority to the first few words in your description, so focus on your main keywords and then elaborate further by using synonyms or other related words.

> META Name: "Keywords"
> General Usage: <META name="Keywords" content="first, second, third"> **COPYRIGHT NOTICE:** When creating keywords for your website, do not infringe on other companies trademarks or copyrights. Many companies have filed and won lawsuits for attempting to "hijack" traffic to competitors from search engines.

Language META Tag (Optional) - The Language META tag declares to users the natural language of the document being indexed. Search engines which index websites based on language often read this tag to determine which language(s) is supported. This tag is particularly useful for non-english and multiple language websites.

HTTP-EQUIV: "Content-Language" Supported Languages: All RFC1766 compliant languages. A small excerpt of available languages is found below:
BG (Bulgarian)
CS (Czech)
DA (Danish)
DE (German)
EL (Greek)
EN (English)
EN-GB (English-Great Britain)
EN-US (English-United States)
ES (Spanish)
ES-ES (Spanish-Spain)
FI (Finnish)
HR (Croatian)
IT (Italian)
FR (French)
FR-CA (French-Quebec)
FR-FR (French-France)
IT (Italian)
JA (Japanese)
KO (Korean)
NL (Dutch)
NO (Norwegian)
PL (Polish)
PT (Portuguese)
RU (Russian)
SV (Swedish)
ZH (Chinese)

General Usage: <META HTTP-EQUIV="Content-Language" content="EN"> Code Generator: Create Language META Tag for me [Click Button Below]

Refresh META Tag (Not Suggested) - Overview: The Refresh Tag defines the number of seconds before refreshing your webpage. The refresh META tag is used as a way to redirect or refresh users to another webpage after X number of seconds. This META tag is often used as a "bridge" page which is accessed first by users and are then redirected to another webpage. Some search engines discourage this type of META tag because it opens opportunity for users to spam search engines with similar pages which all lead to the same page. In addition, this also makes many of the search engines databases cluttered with irrelevant and multiple versions of the same data.

META HTTP-EQUIV: "Refresh"
General Usage: <META HTTP-EQUIV="Refresh" content="X;URL=http://www.website.com/index.html">
Note: X indicates delay in seconds
URL indicates the URL to redirect to

Revisit META Tag (Suggested) - Overview: The Revisit Tag defines how many days the search engine should revisit your webpage. The Revisit META tag defines how often a search engine or spider should come to your website for re-indexing. Often this tag is used for websites that change their content often and on a regular basis. This tag can also be beneficial in boosting your rankings if search engines display results based on the most recent submissions.

META Name: "Revisit-After"
General Usage: <META name="Revisit-After" content="X Days">
Note: X indicates a number

Robots META Tag (Suggested) - Overview: The Robots Tag declares to search engines what content to index and spider. Robots, also known as spiders, are automated mechanisms that spider your

112

site, or search your site on how to categorize the information you submitted to the search engine. Typically, a website owner would submit the main page and the robots would visit your site and collect all subpages and related links from your main page. However, this tag enables you to control which pages you would like spidered, and which to ignore. For instance, certain webpages and directories (ie: CGI Scripts) you may not want indexed in the search engines. Using the robots tag, you can define which pages to follow, which to index and which to ignore completely.

> META Name: "Robots"
> Supported Types: noindex | index | nofollow | follow
> General Usage: <META name="Robots"
> content="index,follow">

Walkthrough – Setting up a HTML page with a META TAG's

1. First thing we must do is locate a FREE Meta tag generator. In the address bar type in "Meta tag generator". You will see a full list of Meta tag generators. A few are:

   > www.submitcorner.com/tools/meta/
   > www.addme.com/meta.htm
   > scrubtheweb.com/abs/builder.html
   > www.free-webmaster-tools.com/meta-tag-generator.htm
   > www.vancouver-webpages.com/meta/mk-metas.html

It does not matter which one you choose, they are almost all similar in function (output).

2. Let's log onto www.seochat.com
3. Scroll down and look for the 'ADVANCED META TAG' function on the left. There is also a link for 'META TAG GENERATOR', which is a much simpler form. The form we will use is:

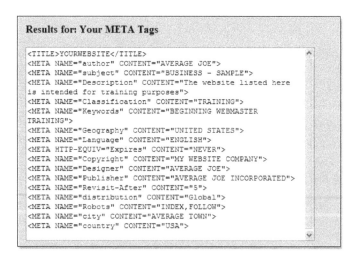

Advanced Meta-Tags Generator Tool
© SEO Chat™

Title
The Title Tag must contain no more than 70 characters (generally, 100 characters may be indexed).

Author
The Author Tag is for the person who wrote the material for the site.

4. This is only the top of the form. The entire form is extremely long. As you can see, it cover's every aspect of a website's information and history.
5. Input as much information into these fields to generate our Meta-Tags. It is not necessary to fill-out all fields.
6. The results will look like the image below:

Results for: Your META Tags

```
<TITLE>YOURWEBSITE</TITLE>
<META NAME="author" CONTENT="AVERAGE JOE">
<META NAME="subject" CONTENT="BUSINESS - SAMPLE">
<META NAME="Description" CONTENT="The website listed here
is intended for training purposes">
<META NAME="Classification" CONTENT="TRAINING">
<META NAME="Keywords" CONTENT="BEGINNING WEBMASTER
TRAINING">
<META NAME="Geography" CONTENT="UNITED STATES">
<META NAME="Language" CONTENT="ENGLISH">
<META HTTP-EQUIV="Expires" CONTENT="NEVER">
<META NAME="Copyright" CONTENT="MY WEBSITE COMPANY">
<META NAME="Designer" CONTENT="AVERAGE JOE">
<META NAME="Publisher" CONTENT="AVERAGE JOE INCORPORATED">
<META NAME="Revisit-After" CONTENT="5">
<META NAME="distribution" CONTENT="Global">
<META NAME="Robots" CONTENT="INDEX,FOLLOW">
<META NAME="city" CONTENT="AVERAGE TOWN">
<META NAME="country" CONTENT="USA">
```

7. *Important – Copy and Paste the Meta Tag data between your HEAD tags on your HTML page.*

8. Use this form or a similar one to create meta tags for every page on your website. This will ensure that all your webpage's get indexed correctly by Search Engine's. Which in turn will lead to more hit's to your site, by people looking for your services.

SETTING UP EMAIL ACCOUNTS

Now that we have our website name (domain) secure, let's proceed to set-up our email. It is important that we have our email account associated with our website. Customers / visitor's are always more at ease contacting you through your business email rather than through other email medians.

Walkthrough – Email Setup

1. Log onto your web host provider. Access your account. If you have chosen to use www.ixwebhosting.com, then your main page (control panel) should look like this....

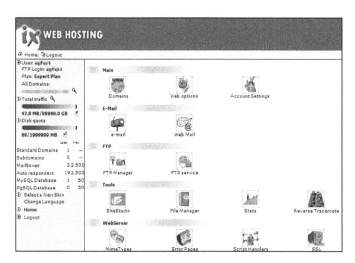

2. Click on the email button. (We may generate as many as 2,500 different email accounts from this one domain if desired)
3. It is here where you can 'ADD NEW EMAIL'. You can also generate a MAILING LIST on the same window, if you desire.

4. Simply fill in the form and feature's you desire to set up your new email.
5. Be sure to keep your password safe.

EMAIL FEATURE'S AVAILABLE

- CATCH ALL - Designate the mailbox to receive messages sent to nonexistent e-mail addresses containing this domain name. For example, somebody sends a message to blablabla@yourdomain.com, which is not a valid e-mail address in your account. By default, this message will bounce back to the sender with an error notification. To have this message land into one of your mailboxes, for example webmaster@yourdomain.com, you should mark this account as *Catch All*. Each account can have only one Catch All mailbox. If you switch it ON for one account, it will go OFF for the old Catch All account.
- DISCARD ALL INCOMING MAIL – Any email's received (spam or not) will be discarded.
- ALIAS BY – By setting up a alias email account (secondary) tied to a primary account, the user may receive all incoming messages from the second email account. For example: primary account 'SAMPLEEMAIL@YOURWEBSITE.COM' also sets up a 'ALIAS BY' account of 'TESTING@YOURWEBSITE.COM'. The user may send out mail using either account as usual. However, incoming mail in the primary and secondary account will ALL go to the primary or 'SAMPLEEMAIL' email without the customer's / respondent's knowledge.
- MAIL FORWARD – All mail forwarded from one email to another automatically.
- AUTORESPONDERS – Are exactly what they sound like. They send back automated messages to incoming mail immediately. You may include a SUBJECT TITLE, SHORT OR LONG MESSAGE AND SEND PICTURES, IMAGES AND OR ANY TYPE FILE YOU WISH.

For example:

Let's say you are selling an eBook and want to have it delivered automatically to your customer's upon payment. By attaching your eBook to the autoresponder email account, anytime a visitor / customer is directed to that email account – your autoresponder will send them back the eBook automatically. This application has not limits and may be used once or a thousand times, once setup. You may also delete and / or modify this autoresponding file at any time.

6. Finally, to access account – Return to your control panel main page (as seen above). Click on the 'WEB MAIL' ICON.

7. Enter your username id and password. Example below:
TESTING@YOURWEBSITE.COM -   username
123456 -   password

PHP SCRIPTS - THE BASICS

There are vast amounts of information written about PHP scripts. PHP stands for Hypertext Preprocessor. PHP is a widely-used general-purpose scripting language that is especially suited for web development and can be embedded into HTML. It generally runs on a web server, taking PHP code as its input and creating web pages as output. It can be deployed on most web servers and on almost every operating system and platform free of charge. PHP is installed on more than 20 million websites and 1 million web servers. As stated in the chapter, "FINDING A GOOD WEB HOST SERVER", It is necessary to have a web host server that runs PHP. Many of the FREE and cheaper Web Host's do not run PHP.

PHP will allow for plain webpage's to become dynamic. They allow interaction between the visitor and webpage. They are scripts (or mini-programs) running in the background to aid the user to search for zip codes, take tests and quizzes, set password protection for webpage's, manage mailing lists and much more.

PHP may be implemented in two forms.

- PHP scripts may consist of entire webpage's.

  For example: In the Simple PHP Test below, we have written three lines of code and saved the page in the PHP format. When we call upon the page, the mini-program runs giving us the result.

Simple PHP Test

Open your text editor. Open a blank page and title it TESTING. Save it as a PHP file as shown below:

119

Enter your HTML view and clear all contents except the following :

1. **< ? php**
2. **echo " Hello World ! " ;**
3. **? >**

Upload   file   to   your   website.   Open
www.yourwebsite.com/testing.php. Should look like this:

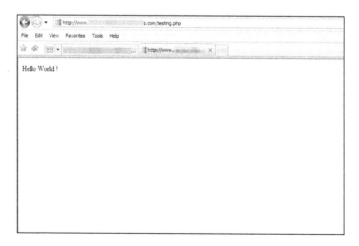

- PHP scripts may also be copied and pasted directly into an HTML document to produce the same result. However, the HTML document may also have additional PHP scripts, RSS

120

Feeds and website FORMS to gather information from visitors as well.

The example below show us the simple procedure of pasting the same 3 lines of code directly into our HTML document.

COMBINING HTML and PHP

It is also possible to integrate php scripts directly into html documents. As seen below, the process is quite simple. PHP will function normally, as long as the HTML tags are outside the PHP start and end tags, as shown below.

```
1.  < html >
2.  < head >
3.  < title > sample php script < / title >
4.  < / head >
5.  < body >
6.  < b >
7.  < ? php
8.        echo " Hello World ! " ;
9.  ? >
10. < / b>
11. < / body >
12. < / html >
```

FREE & PAID PHP SCRIPTS

While there are thousands of free scripts to choose from, there are also many companies pushing their scripts for sale. Most of these scripts are relatively simple to integrate into our website. The scripts plug directly into our HTML. It is important to understand that PHP scripts will not show up in your PREVIEW page on your HTML editor. PHP scripts require the internet to run. Therefore, after you plug in your script (s), save and upload your webpage. Go to that page directly and you will see the script at work.

As with most things on the internet, there are many items for sale. PHP scripts are one of those items. However, there are also thousands of FREE php scripts we may download and use freely as well. Go down these lists to see if any of these free scripts could help your website along. Some of the categories for these scripts include:

- Ad Management
- Affiliate Programs
- Auctions
- Blog
- Bookmark Management
- Calculators
- Calendars
- Chat Scripts
- Classified Ads
- Click Tracking
- Communication Tools
- Content Management
- Contests and Awards
- Countdowns
- Counters
- Customer Support
- Database Tools
- Date and Time
- Development Tools
- Discussion Boards
- Documents
- E-Commerce
- Education
- Email Systems
- Error Handling
- Exchanges
- FAQ and Knowledgebase
- File Manipulation
- Financial Tools
- Flash and PHP
- Form Processors
- Games and Entertainment
- Graphs and Charts
- Groupware Tools
- Guestbooks
- Healthcare
- Image Galleries
- Image Handling
- Interactive Stories
- Link Checking
- Link Indexing
- Mailing List Managers
- Match Making

- Miscellaneous
- Multi-Level Marketing
- Multimedia
- Music Libraries
- Networking Tools
- News Publishing
- Open Directory Project
- Organizers
- Polls and Voting
- Portal Systems
- Postcards
- Quote Display
- Randomizing
- Real Estate
- Redirection
- Reviews and Ratings
- Search Engines
- Security Systems
- Server Management
- Site Mapping
- Site Navigation
- Site Recommendation
- Software Repository
- Tests and Quizzes
- Text Processing
- Top Sites
- URL Submitters
- Usenet Gateway
- User Authentication
- User Management
- Vertical Markets
- Virtual Communities
- WAP and WML
- Web Fetching
- Web Hosting Tools
- Web Rings
- Web Search
- Web Traffic Analysis
- Wikis
- WYSIWYG Editors
- XML and PHP
- Zip Code Locators

MORE PHP INFO

The typical php file is a script or mini-program lying dormant upon your web host server until called upon. Once activated or called upon, the script will run and produce the output. Depending on the type of script we are working with, the results will vary. However the process is the same.

Let's look at the simple form below. Even though the form looks simple to the eye, it requires a good bit of HTML programming. In the first step, we will setup the actual form. Then, once the SUBMIT button is pressed, the PHP script will activate. In this form, the information will be validated and sent to the email of our choice.

It is important to understand that, the HTML page alone will not produce results. In this case, an email of the information the user wants to convey to us. without the PHP script, the information (Name, Email Address, Postal Address and any Message) that the user has just filled in will basically just sit there on the users screen and be lost once he moves to another website.

It is the PHP script that will validate and send the information in the form to our email immediately upon pressing of the SUBMIT button.

SOME BASIC PHP STEPS

To start your PHP scripts you need to use the PHP tags, these tags will tell the server that what is inside the tags needs to be parsed by the PHP engine before it's output is displayed. The opening and closing tags are shown below.

```
<?php // opening PHP tag
/*
```

everthing between the two tags (parts in blue)
will be parsed by PHP and then the output will be
displayed in the browser.
*/

// closing PHP tag -> ?>

Comments

See the orange text in the example above? Those are comments.
Comments allow you to leave yourself notes or reminders while
you're coding. They're also useful in situations where you are
working with multiple programmers. You can create either single
line comments or multiple line comments.

To make a single line comment just type "//", all of text after that, on
the same line be commented out. You can also use the "#" character
to create single line comments.

To create multiple line comments type "/*" followed by your
comments, then type "*/" when you want to end your commenting.

Basic Echo

One of the most basic things you should know how to do with PHP
is a simple echo. by 'an echo' I mean printing out text to the page. To
do this, we'll use the built in PHP function, <u>echo</u>. Here's an example:

```
<?php

// Make sure to end every line with a semicolon!(;)

echo "Text in these quotes will show up on the page. ";
echo 'You can also use single quotes to echo text. ';

// You can also use the print function
```

```php
print "print and echo do the same thing. ";
print "It's up to you which one you want to use.";

?>
```

If you are using double quotes to write your text and you want print out double quotes, you need to escape them. To do this just put a "\" before your quotes. Do the same if you want to print out a single quote when you are using single quotes for the echo. I know that sounds a bit confusing, so here's an example:

```php
<?php

// escape the double quotes

echo "The name of this tutorial is \"PHP Basics\".";

// escape the single quote

echo 'Hopefully it\'s been good so far.';

?>
```

It's important to remember to escape your quotes when necessary, something as small as that can sometimes be the cause of PHP parse errors that make you want to just pull out all of your hair.

Variables

If you've studied algebra, then you've come across variables before. Variables are used in PHP too, they're used to hold values. To create a variable, just type a dollar sign($) followed by your variable name, an equal sign(=) and the value you want it to hold. Here's an example:

```php
<?php

// Let's stick some text in a variable.

$myText = "This text is now held in a variable.";

// That's easy, how about a number?

$myNumber = 87;

?>
```

Notice, I didn't use quotes when declaring the $myNumber variable. When assigning an integer, quotes may be used, but aren't required.

Now that these variables are defined, you can use them later in your scripts, simply by calling upon the variables, here's an example:

```php
<?php

// output the contents of the variable $myText

echo $myText.'<br />';

echo '19'.$myNumber.'<br />'; // will output '1987'

?>
```

The period after '19' is used in PHP as a concatenation operator, which means that the '87', held in $myNumber will be combined, or connected, with the '19', then the result (1987) is echoed.

One important thing to remember about variables is that they **are** case-sensitive, which means $myvar and $myVar are two completely different variables. It's also important to remember that variable names cannot start with numbers. They may only start with underscores(_) and letters. However, they may contain any combination of letters, numbers, and underscores after that.

CREATING A SIMPLE FEEDBACK FORM

Setting up a form for use with a PHP script is exactly the same as normal in HTML. As this is a PHP tutorial I will not go into depth in how to write your form but I will show you three of the main pieces of code you must know:

```
<input type="text" name="thebox" value="Your Name">
```

Will display a text input box with Your Name written in it as default. The value section of this code is optional. The information defined by name will be the name of this text box and should be unique.

```
<textarea name="message">
Please write your message here.
</textarea>
```

Will display a large scrolling text box with the text 'Please write your message here.' as default. Again, the name is defined and should be unique.

```
<input type="submit" value="Submit">
```

This will create a submit button for your form. You can change what it says on the button by changing the button's value.

All the elements for your form must be enclosed in the <form> tags. They are used as follows:

```
<form action="process.php" method="post">
Form elements and formatting etc.
</form>
```

The form's action tells it what script to send its data to (in this case its process.php). This can also be a full URL (e.g. http://www.mysite.com/scripts/private/processors/process.php). The method tells the form how to submit its data. POST will send the data in a data stream to the script when it is requested. GET is the other option. GET will send the form data in the form of the url so it would appear after a question mark e.g. http://www.mysite.com/process.php?name=david

It really makes no difference which system you use but it is normally better to use POST if you are using passwords or sensitive information as they should not be shown in the browser's address bar.

Getting The Form Information

The next step is to get the data the form has submitted into your script so that you can do something with it. This is. There are basically two different methods of getting the data into PHP, which depend on how they were submitted. There are two submission methods, GET and POST, which can both be used by forms. The difference between the two is that using GET, the variables and data will be shown in the page address, but using POST it is invisible. The benefit of GET, though is that you can submit information to the script without a form, by simply editing the URL.

This works the same as submitting a form using GET. The advantage of this is that you can create links to your scripts which do different things depending on the link clicked. For example you could create a script which will show different pages depending on the link clicked:

yourpage.php?user=david

could show David's page and:

yourpage.php?user=tom

could show Tom's page, using the same script.

It is also possible to pass more than one piece of information to the script using this system by separating them with the & symbol:

yourpage.php?user=david&referrer=gowansnet&area=6

These could all be accessed separately using the GET variables user, referrer and area.

To get a variable which has been sent to a script using the POST method you use the following code:

$variablename=$_POST['variable'];

which basically takes the variable from the POST (the name of a form field) and assigns it to the variable $variablename.

Similarly, if you are using the GET method you should use the form:

$variablename=$_GET['variable'];

This should be done for each variable you wish to use from your form (or URL).

Creating The Form To Mail Script

To finish off this section, I will show you how to use what you have learnt in this part and the last to create a system which will e-mail a user's comments to you.

Firstly, create this form for your HTML page:

```
<form action="mail.php" method="post">
Your Name: <input type="text" name="name"><br>
E-mail: <input type="text" name = "email"><br><br>
Comments<br>
<textarea name="comments"></textarea><br><br>
<input type="submit" value="Submit">
</form>
```

This will make a simple form where the user can enter their e-mail address, their name and their comments. You can, of course, add extra parts to this form but remember to update the script too. Now create the PHP script:

```
<?
function checkOK($field)
{
if (eregi("\r",$field) || eregi("\n",$field)){
die("Invalid Input!");
}
}

$name=$_POST['name'];
checkOK($name);
$email=$_POST['email'];
checkOK($email);
$comments=$_POST['comments'];
checkOK($comments);
$to="php@yourwebsite.com";
$message="$name just filled in your comments form. They
```

said:\n$comments\n\nTheir e-mail address was: $email";
if(mail($to,"Comments From Your Site",$message,"From: $email\n")) {
echo "Thanks for your comments.";
} else {
echo "There was a problem sending the mail. Please check that you filled in the form correctly.";
}
?>

Remember to replace php@yourwebsite.com with your own e-mail address. This script should be saved as mail.php and both should be uploaded. Now, all you need to do is to fill in your comments form.

The first part of that script may look a bit strange:

```
function checkOK($field)
{
if (eregi("\r",$field) || eregi("\n",$field)){
die("Invalid Input!");
}
}
```

You don't really need to worry about what this is doing, but basically, it stops spammers from using your form to send thier spam messages by checking special characters are not present in the input which can be used to trick the computer into sending messages to other addresses. It is a fuction which checks for these characters, and if they are found, stops running the script.

The lines:

checkOK($name);

etc. run this check on each input to ensure it is valid

Other PHP resource websites include:

www.scripts.com
www.php-scripts.com
www.scriptsbank.com
www.gscripts.net
www.sitescripts.com
www.hot-php-scripts.com
www.php.net
www.dbscripts.net
www.free-php.net
www.opensourcescripts.com/dir/php/

FUN & EASY TO INSTALL SCRIPTS

PASSWORD PROTECT WEB PAGES'

This FREE script will present user with password entry form, and will not let visitor see your private content without providing a password. Multiple user accounts support, improved security, automatic logout, and manual logout feature. Highly rated FREE script provided by **zubrag.com**. Complete walkthrough for easy setup and install. Download script page: http://www.zubrag.com/scripts/password-protect.php.

CREATE A DIRECTORY

Create a general directory of the best resources accross the web, and allow people to submit their sites. You can also earn money by charging for the review process, as well as a premium for featured links. Many have profitted from this model, and people continue to do this today.

Create a directory centered around your niche. Maybe you already have a website about a topic you know well, and you want to create a well organized link section to help your users find the best resources in your niche neatly organized into categories. phpLD can be a great way to bring better organization to your links, and also also make it possible for your users to submit their favorite links.

Create a regional directory. This is pretty big right now, and many are getting in on this, because people are finding ways to build a local directory and profit from it. You can make a directory for your town or city, and then you can promote it, and even sell advertising. Visit link to download script:
http://www.phplinkdirectory.com/articlescript/phpLD_version_2.php

CREATE AN IMAGE GALLERY

Gallery is an open source project with the goal to develop and support **leading photo sharing web application solutions**.

The Gallery project develops open source software licensed under the GPL, and is maintained and developed by a community of users and developers. The development is a distributed effort, with collaboration from around the globe. The team is well organized, with weekly meetings, and constant communication. Serving millions worldwide, the Gallery project is the most widely used system of its kind. Gallery is free to download and use. Visit: http://gallery.menalto.com

CREATE YOUR OWN BLOG

On this site you can download and install a FREE software script called WordPress. To do this you need a **web host** who meets the **minimum requirements** and a little time. WordPress is **completely customizable** and can be used for almost anything. There is also a **service** called **WordPress.com** which lets you get started with a new and free WordPress-based blog in seconds, but varies in several ways and is less flexible than the WordPress you download and install yourself. Visit: http://wordpress.org/

CREATING EASY TO USE FORMS

USING PHP vs. ONLINE FORM GENERATORS

PHP FORMS

Add an email form to your website within a minute with my PHP mailer script so that your customers can contact you by email quickly and easily. The script is fully customizable by editing a simple configuration file - even a chimp could do it!

A huge amount of people use web based email services such as Hotmail and Yahoo. If they want to get in touch with you by email, instead of being able to simply click an email link (like users with email clients such as Outlook), they have to go to the email providers website - log in to their account - create a new email - copy your email address across and then finally send the email.

That is a bit of a long way round when you could have a simple form for them to fill in and send to you, so you should have an email form on your website to make it more user friendly for your visitors/potential customers

- Simple set up by editing config file
- Allows for easy language changes using the config file
- Friendly error messages for if the script is installed incorrectly
- Users prompted to enter random validation code to avoid automated submissions (which are invariably spam of some sort)
- Ideal for anyone with little or no knowledge of PHP, as there is no script editing involved

Output -- >

This FREE php Form is posted through BELLONLINE.CO.UK.COM. It also comes with a VALIDATION CODE requirement, thus eliminating those pesky form bots from spamming your email.

This forms download address is: www.bellonline.co.uk/download.php?file=1. The download should consist of these files.

- README.TXT
- DEMO.PHP
- CONFIG.PHP
- BELLMAILER.PHP

Simply open the README file and begin configuring your files. This FORM is highly customizable. Please pay close attention to the "CONFIGURATION" section of the readme file. Once completed, install the BELLMAILER.PHP into your HTML document or template page as the README file states (placement depends on your preference) and that's it. I recommend you set up a blank (dummy) HTML or template page to test it out first. Remember, it is vital to have a web host server that runs PHP. The low budget web host's do not. Always backup your 'GOOD' HTML pages.

Now save and upload your CONFIG.PHP, BELLMAILER.PHP and the HTML document you inserted the script into.

ONLINE FORM GENERATORS (STORAGE)

Zoho Creator *beta* is one of the best FREE form creator's & storage on the internet. They're 'App Builder" is a state of the art FORM building system, allowing you to Using online form generators / storage sites are very beneficial, especially if you do not have a web host server that runs PHP.

Let's begin by logging onto they're website. www.creator.zoho.com. Currently, this site and all it's goodies are running in beta mode, which means they are testing and everything is FREE. They have many options to choose from, in aiding our development of our website. We will be working with their web form builder (located under the overview button) on the homepage. If you have not already done so, go ahead and signup for a free account – 100% free. At your main page you will see the Create New Application button as seen below.

Online Form Setup - Walkthrough

Setting Up a Simple Form - Create New Application

1. Once you are logged in, click on the

    Create New Application »

    button displayed on the top-right corner.

2. You will be given three different formats of FORMS to create as seen here.

3. Select the **Add form** option to create a custom application from scratch by adding blank forms.

4. We now need to choose an application name. It may be anything. Let's choose **My Contacts,** and form name as **New Contact.** The form name may also be named anything you would like.

5. Now, you may select to use the **Create From Scratch** option to create your application or use a prefabricated form **(Use Form Template)** from zoho creator. Let's work with the former.

6. Select the time zone relevant to your locale from **Time Zone** dropdown menu.

7. Click **Create Now** to create the application.

An application created in Zoho Creator can either be public or private. All forms and views in a public application is accessible by public visitors. A private application can be accessed only if the owner of the application shares it with specific users, from the Share tab. By default, an application created in Zoho Creator is private.

Note: **public** or **private**.

137

8. The My Contacts application is created with a blank **New Contact form,** as shown in the screen-shot given below:

9. *Next step is very easy. Setting up the form. Just **click** on the item you would like to add to your form from the list on the left (blue buttons) and drag & drop in the blank field to the right.*

Let's drag and drop the Single Line Text Field. Label Name : **Name** (for example). Click Done

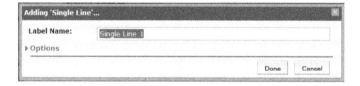

Drag and drop the E-mail field type, specify the Label Name as **Email Address** and click **Done.**

Drag and drop the Number field, specify the Label Name as **Contact Number** and click **Done.**

Now, you have your Contact form ready for users to submit their data. You can customize your form, field and label widths by selecting **More Actions -> Form Properties**, from the form header.

7. The form will save all information input Click on the VIEWS button to observe the information that has been input. This is where we may adjust our form output. Display Properties, Column properties & widths may be adjusted, etc.

Customize Application Layout and Themes

Once you have your Forms and Views configured, you can use the **Customize** tab to customize the layout and theme for your application.

- Select **Choose Layout**
- Select a layout of our choice, from the variety of layouts displayed. For example, let us select the **Tab layout** as shown in the screen-shot below.

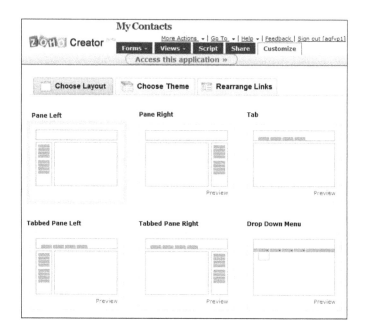

- By default, the form/view will be displayed under the **Home tab**. You can click on the **Rearrange Links** option to change the tab name or to add new sections and rearrange your form/views the new tab/sections, as shown below. Here, we have added a new section named **Add New Contact** and placed the "New Contact" form under this section. Similarly, we have placed the New Contact view under a new section named **View Contacts**.

- Select **Choose Theme** to apply a theme for the Contacts application.
- Select a theme of our choice, from the variety of themes displayed. By default, the Classic theme will be applied to the form/views.
- For example, let us select the **Gradient theme** with the required color and click on **Apply** to apply the theme.
- You can also create customized themes by selecting the **Custom Themes** button.

Access the Application & Upload to Your Website

Now, let us switch on to the **Access mode** of the **My Contacts** application, to submit data to the New Contact form and view the submitted data. To go to access mode and submit data,

Click on  button. This is what you should see:

Click on the MORE ACTIONS button:

Click on the EMBED IN YOUR WEBSITE button. You will be given two choices of how you will want to access your form.

- First, the **IFRAME SNIPPET,** will create a small box inside your website (allow a window from your website to connect directly to Creator Zoho). This iFrame will allow the user to imput his NAME, EMAIL ADDRESS & CONTACT NUMBER directly from your website into your online form. Creator Zoho will them store that information for you indefinitely or until you delete.
    - Simply copy and paste the entire code from <iframe height> to </iframe>. Place the code in the exact location of your website that you desire. Remember, you may alter or modify the website form to blend in with your website as desired.

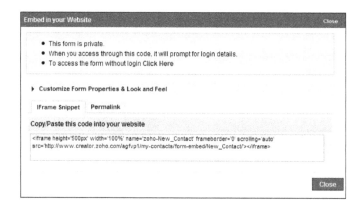

- Second, you will be given a short **PERMALINK** code. This code or hyperlink will point your web visitor to a clean page with your form on it. For example: You can have a statement, such as: CONTACT FORM – CLICK HERE and embed or establish a hyperlink (http://www.creator.zoho.com/yourwebsite.com/form-perma/New_Contact/) pointing to the form below.

You may access, modify and/or create additional forms in the same manner. Simply log into your Creator Zoho profile to view any NEW CONTACTS that you may have picked up. You may also set up a email notification when visitors use your form. Especially handy if you use a smart phone device (Blackberry).

KEYWORDS

Embedding your website with relevant keywords

Keywords are a list of words and phrases that help search engines index your website. When someone is searching for information on the web, they will usually visit a search engine and type in some words describing what they are looking for. The search engine then checks its database and returns the results listing pages that meet the words submitted.

Keywords are important as they can be used successfully in conjunction with the search engines to provide you with a free source of targeted traffic to your web site. They enable people who need your product, service or information to find you. Appropriate keywords are like a telephone number for your business and the search engine is like the telephone book – it lists your name and number.

So, how do you determine what keywords are relevant for your site? Firstly, you need to put yourself in your potential customer's shoes to determine what words they would submit to the search engine when they are looking for you. Also, review your web site pages and pick out key phrases and words that describe your business, product or service.

List these words and phrases as they will form the basis for optimizing your web pages so that they will rank higher on the search engines. The more specific your keywords the better. Remember that single word keywords will have a lot more competition for top ranking search results than phrases.

Don't expect that the identification of your keywords and the submission of your pages to the search engines to result in an immediate flood of traffic to your site. Firstly, many of the search engines take a number of weeks to process your submission. Secondly, some search engines rank based on a number of factors including site popularity.

The number of sites that link to your site determines site popularity. Therefore, to improve your site popularity will require a reciprocal links strategy.

The appropriate choice of keywords combined with optimized web pages submitted to the search engines can result in free targeted traffic to your site. This is a source of traffic that should not be overlooked.

A simple technique to embed your website with relevant keywords is BEING OBVIOUS. Fill your text with the keywords that describe your website. Customers / Visitors are not patient when searching the internet. If they are drawn to a particular website that inaccurately has too many of the wrong keywords in its main page, they will be on that website less than 5 seconds. If you are in the business of selling cell phones, for example, input the words "cell phone, phones" repeatedly. It is also a good idea to list the styles and different vendors you carry, i.e. "AT&T, VERIZON, SPRINT" etc.

A more advanced embedding technique also is possible. What I like to call Invisible Embedding or IE. IE is used when your code-to-text ratio is too low. The Code to Text Ratio represents the percentage of actual text in a web page. This is important because search engines and spiders calculate the relevancy of a web page based on a high code to text ratio. The higher the code, the better chance of getting a good page ranking for your page.

The average Code to Text is 0 – 10%. Excellent code has a > 25% text ratio.

- Invisible Embedding Walkthrough

Open a Floating Layer on your Web Editor (pre-upload). Fill that floating box with as many words as you would like. Should look like below.

```
Cell phone, phones, Verizon, Sprint,
AT&T, Cell phone, phones, Verizon,
Sprint, AT&T, Cell phone, phones,
Verizon, Sprint, AT&T, Cell phone,
phones, Verizon, Sprint, AT&T, Cell
phone, phones, Verizon, Sprint,
AT&T, Cell phone, phones, Verizon,
Sprint, AT&T, Cell phone, phones,
Verizon, Sprint, AT&T, Cell phone,
phones, Verizon, Sprint, AT&T, Cell
phone, phones, Verizon, Sprint,
AT&T, Cell phone, phones, Verizon,
Sprint, AT&T, Cell phone, phones,
Verizon, Sprint, AT&T, Cell phone,
phones, Verizon, Sprint, AT&T, Cell
phone, phones, Verizon, Sprint,
AT&T, Cell phone, phones, Verizon,
Sprint, AT&T, Cell phone, phones,
Verizon, Sprint, AT&T, Cell phone,
phones, Verizon, Sprint, AT&T, Cell
phone, phones, Verizon, Sprint,
AT&T, Cell phone, phones, Verizon,
Sprint, AT&T, Cell phone, phones,
Verizon, Sprint, AT&T, Cell phone,
phones, Verizon, Sprint, AT&T,
```

As you can see I has entered the same words multiple times (separated only by a comma...no periods). The box may be as narrow or wide as you wish. Play with the amount of repeated keywords to get your code-to-ratio up. Use SEOCHAT.COM to keep checking your ratio. They have a convenient code-to-ratio checker on the left of their main page. Now we will instruct the box to exist somewhere off screen where neither you nor your customers will ever see or detect it.

Search engines will see this text and cache the words and your code to text ratio. Next, highlight your floating box and right click. Enter your LAYER PROPERTIES. Should look like this:

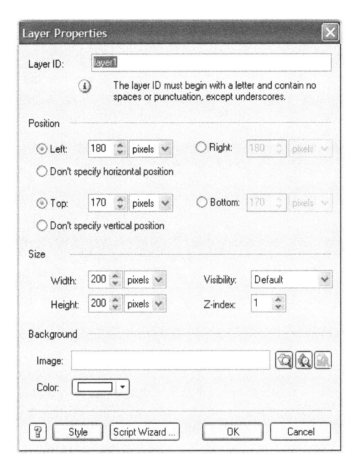

Under Position, enter -5000 LEFT and -5000 TOP. The box will exist waaaay off screen. That's it. If you need to bring it back, just use your admin to find how many floating boxes you have and highlight (double-click). That will bring the LAYER PROPERTIES box back. Then enter 100 Left and 100 Top, to bring back into view.

PUTTING YOUR WEBSITE ON THE MAP

PUTTING YOUR WEBSITE ON THE MAP

Search Engine Usage for May 2008 – Over 7.8 Billion searches were made. Over 90 % of those searches were made using 4 website's (according to Nielson/Net Ratings). They are Google.com, Yahoo.com, MSN.com and AOL.com.

Search Engine	Share of Searches
Google	59.3%
Yahoo	16.9%
MSN	13.3%
AOL	4.1%

Now that you have completed your website and have it uploaded onto the internet, we need to put your website on the map. We will begin by introducing your site to the following search engine companies – Google & Yahoo.

Imagine your website as a small dot in outer-space. You may have a new and revolutionary website with important information that thousands of people will use and enjoy. You may even be the next Google, **YouTube** or **FaceBook**. How will everyone find you? Search Engine's and Directories!

Internet search engines are special sites on the Web that are designed to help people find information stored on other sites. There are differences in the ways various search engines work, but they all perform three basic tasks:

- They search the Internet -- or select pieces of the Internet -- based on important words (keywords).
- They keep an index of the words they find, and where they find them.

- They allow users to look for words or combinations of words found in that index.

Search engine's cache (store) information that is on your website. Later, when users are searching for an item and or information on the internet – the search engines will look into their stores of information and list the most relevant website's (based on what **keywords** that the user is searching for – discussed in depth in the KEYWORDS chapter). The order of which website is displayed first depends mainly on your PR (Page Rank).

Page Rank: Was devised by Google. It measures not only how many links point to a website, but the "quality" of the sites providing the links. Discussed in the next chapter – BOOSTING PAGERANK.

Registering with the Major Search Engine's & Directories

- Google
- Yahoo
- MSN
- Alta Vista
- Alltheweb
- DMOZ

GOOGLE

(This section is similar to the SITEMAP chapter, however necessary due to the fact that people may have skipped that chapter – submitting your website to these search engines is critical to gaining exposure to internet traffic.)

Let's begin by connecting to the internet and logging onto GOOGLE.COM. At the top right of the screen you will see the SIGN IN hyperlink. Click on it.

You should now be at the Google Accounts page. Here click "CREATE ONE FOR FREE" link in the middle of the page, just above the Gmail button.

Next step, filling in the form to create our FREE Google account. Be sure not to forget your email and password. You will be using it a few hundred times within the following months. I suggest you write it down on a post-it and attach it to your screen. Be sure to use a good email, as you will have to click on a link sent there to activate your account. Click on the email link and your account will be active.

As you can see, there are many other things you can do with your GOOGLE account & all for FREE. Signup for Gmail, Adsense, Adwords, Alerts, Groups and more. We will be using the Adsense & Adwords features later in the book to advertise and generate income on our website.

Enter the following link to Submit your website into GOOGLE's directory.
http://www.google.com/submit_content.html

Fill-out the form and submit. This will add your website into the largest search engine in the world. Congratulations! You have started the ball rolling on promoting your website. What GOOGLE will do within the next couple of days is send it's robot or google-bot to take a quick picture of your website and cache it for search for all it's users later. That means millions of users everyday may be looking for what you are promoting.

Now that the robot or google-bot is on it's way to check out our site, let's make sure to make it easy for him to find (or not) exactly what we want him to find.

You may be asking yourself, why did I register an account with GOOGLE, all I had to do was go to the link directly. That is true. However, in order to promote your website effectively, certain extra steps must be made that many people do not know about.

ADD SITE – https://www.google.com/webmasters/tools/dashboard

Your GOOGLE account is now connected directly with your website. As you can see from the image below, GOOGLE has just accessed your home page and page's from your site are included in their index.

Let's VERIFY OUR SITE. The easiest way to do this is to upload a html file. Simply, upload a blank page onto your root or main ftp page of your web host server and name it exactly the GOOGLE html provided. The page will be blank and the name should look like this: google42342lljl324kj324.html

Once you have done this, go back to the verification page and click on the Verify button. You have just shown GOOGLE that you have a new website and are serious about promoting it.

Now let's help GOOGLE bot a little more by uploading our Sitemap and Robot.txt files. Click on the sitemaps tab on the left.

Click on ADD A SITEMAP. On the drop down "Choose type", we will be uploading a General Web Sitemap. We should have already created a Sitemap in the supported format and uploaded it to our web host server (previous chapters). Type in the name and location of the sitemap file. For example:

http://www.yourwebsite.com/sitemap.txt

Let's inspect the sitemaps page now. We have just added our sitemap and GOOGLE acknowledges that and states that it may take several hours to update. This is true. GOOGLE is fantastic in all their FREE applications they offer, however, they are a bit slow though.

Under Sitemap stats (above the ADD A SITEMAP link) you will see that you have
Total URL's - 0

This is normal. GOOGLE will visit your site and begin caching your website a little bit at a time. They do not usually record the whole site at one time. My past experience has shown me that a website of 20 pages or more takes about 2-4 weeks to cache completely.
It is important that we provide GOOGLE with a sitemap, because we do not want them to miss any web page that we have spent time on. It would be a shame to build a beautiful and productive webpage and have noone know of its existence.

Let's check back in a day or two to see if they have began caching our site. Remember to look at the TOTAL URL's cached.

Sitemap stats
Total URLs: 0

Click on the TOOLS button to make sure your ROBOT.TXT file upload correctly. You should see your robot.txt file information in the box. Status should be 200 (success) without any errors on the top. If any errors exist, be sure of the placement of the robot text file. It should be on your root or www.yourwebsite.com/robot.txt. Example:

User-Agent: *
Disallow: /cgi-bin/
Disallow: /images/

We can adjust and tweak our website to strengthen our weak points by using the other tools as well -- Diagnostics, Statistics and Links. Return often to inspect these parameters of your website and see what you need to clean up on your website. The smoother your partnership with GOOGLE the better your results will be in attracting new customers – FREE of charge.

YAHOO

The next major search engine we want to introduce our site to is YAHOO.COM.
There are two approach's we may follow in submitting to Yahoo.com. The first entails submitting our website as a guest. The second approach is to sign in to Yahoo as a regular member/user of their system.

Submitting as a guest

In submitting our website as a guest, we will simply go to the correct webpage and enter our website name and forget it. Yahoo will search and cache their findings. Type in the following link --

http://search.yahoo.com/info/submit.html. The following page should appear.

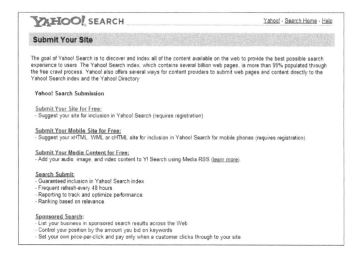

Click on the "SUBMIT YOUR SITE FOR FREE" link. Next click on the "SUBMIT A WEBSITE OR WEBPAGE" link.

You should be here....

That's it. Your website has been submitted.

Member Submittal of a Website

I recommend submitting your website via this method. You may track one or multiple website's you are working on, correct any problem's that may arise in your website caching, use the webmaster tools (free of charge) to promote your site via gadgets that yahoo supplies and more.

To go directly to the login page type in --
https://siteexplorer.search.yahoo.com

The following will appear. Bookmark this page for future reference. You will be coming here practically everyday for the next several weeks. Also, be sure to write down your username and password somewhere accessible. If your like me, you have several id's and passwords spread out across the internet and remembering them all is practically impossible.

Click on *My Sites* (top left of page)

Once you have logged in you will have the option to submit your website. If you don't have an id yet, go ahead and set one up now.

Once you have put in your website, you may track it through this portal. View your "New sites, Authentication, Pending and Failed/Problem Sites". You may view who you are linking to and who is linking to you. Via Preferences you can set up an email account with your login id. Set up a Blog via your website for promotion. Download and attach Badges directly to your website with Yahoo Inbound Links Information. Sign-up for Web Service API's to further promote your website.

Yahoo is great for offering outstanding user support and webmaster tools and options for website promotion. Once you have streamlined your website and smoothed out all wrinkles with Yahoo you will be on your way to getting increased traffic and a higher website ranking.

MORE SECRETS, TIPS & TRICKS

MORE SECRETS, TIPS & TRICKS

Acquiring Quality Links To Your Website – FREE

Listed below are several hundred FREE website's you may submit your site to. Most of them are directories with good PR. As a beginning webmaster with a brand new website it is a bit tough to acquire the quality links to our website that we want right off the bat. We are going to put in a little elbow grease to build our site up. The rationale behind this is that quality website's are not motivated to link to website's with a lower PR (Page Rank) than their own. If they link to too many of these sites they will lose their ranking as well. For example: a website that has a PR 2 will require that any and all reciprocal links (two way links to and from the original website) have a PR2 or greater. You will run into many of these site's. It is important that you remember this and play the same game when you are at bat.

Once your website begins climbing in rank you will begin receiving emails from these web promotion individuals regarding link exchanges. I receive multiple requests per week and politely decline to exchange with them.

My PR3 and PR5 sites will lose too much ranking if I link to these websites with PR0 or No Ranking at all (due to newness).

The best link generating networks that require little or no effort and supply multiple inbound links include:

Linkshighway.net   Free-linkexchange.net
Linkmarket.net   Autolinkmanager.com
Linktradeexchange.com   Linkdiary.com
Automaticbacklinks.com   Linktopia.org
Linkwizard.net   Megalinksexchange.com

Submit your website to the following FREE directories. Definitely time consuming, but worth it.

a1dir.com	hanja.info
a2adir.info	himalyan.net
a2zwebindex.com	hits2u.com
aapkachoice.com	homesalediy.com
aardvark.co.za	hotlaunch.com
aaspaas.com	ibratu.ws
abacho.co.uk	idofind.com
abacus.com	iftekharkhan.com
abcrealestatedirectory.com	ilinkr.com
abizdirectory.com	illumirate.com
acoon.com	infiniteinfo.net
activerain.com	infotiger.com
addgoodsites.com	intelseek.com
addlinkyour.com	inter-change.com
addsearch.com	internetweblist.info
addyoursite.org	interweblinks.com
addyoururl.biz	irealestatedirectory.com
admcity.com	irealweb.com
aeiwi.com	jayde.com
aeonity.ocm	jblue.cjb.net
aesop.com	jewana.com
agreatrealestate.com	jorgensenterprises.com
alexa.com	khoj.com
alinkpop.com	klingelton-tipp.com
alistdirectory.com	krstarica.com
alistsites.com	landdirectory.com
alu2.com	lazymule.info
americasbest.com	linkaddurl.com
americasbestmortgage.us	linkdirectory.com
amfibi.com	linkmarket.net
amidalla.com	linkmaster.com
amray.com	linkof.net
anaximanderdirectory.com	link-professor.com
annutitiesnet.com	links.maxxfusion.com
anybrowser.com	links.scrabblestop.com
arabji.com	links4homes.com
arakco.com	linkscatalog.net
arakne-links.com	linkscout.com
articletrader.com	linksdirectory.org.uk
artoolinks.com	linkshighway.net
averlo.com	link-trinity.com
awebindex.com	linktrix.com
awned.com	loadzalinks.com
bamdirectory.com	lookdirectory.com
beamed.com	massivenetlinks.com
bedwan.com	mavicanet.com

bertaphil.com	maxxlinks.com
bestdirectory4you.com	megri.com
bestwebdirectory.info	mericlong.net
bestwwws.com	meta-search-engine.info
bestyellow.com	minutedirectory.com
bhanvad.com	mixcat.com
bigday-us.com	modynet.net
bizahead.com	mxdu.com
bizfire-directory.com	myprowler.com
blajob.com/partners1.php	nameplot.com
bluchang.com	nameproz.com
bmeta.com	national-real-estate-directory
bpubs.com	nenib.com
brainfind.com	netdung.com
bridgeloan.biz	newworldproducts.org
businessseek.biz	nhuu.com
busybits.com	nimadirectory.com
c2000.com	nonar.com
cafrid.com	ofree.net
campusti.org	onedir.biz
can links	onemission.com
canadiancontent.net	one-sublime-directory.com
championdirectory.info	onlinedirectoryweb.info
changing links	onlinedirectoryworld.com
choiceww.com	oodir.com
classicdirectory.info	opdir.com
claymont.com	pawei.com
click.pk	pedsters-planet.co.uk
clickre.com	pegasusdirectory.com
clicky.com	projectultra.com
cmpcmm.com	property-directory.org
codot.net	qualitylinksdirect.com
commercialcentral.com	qmeo.com
comoestamos.com	rdirectory.net
coolpick.com	real.estategateway.com
coolseller.co.uk	realestateabc.com
costaricaclick.com	real-estate-agents.com
craigwbrown.com	realestatebusinessdirectory.com
crispyweb.com	realestatediscuss.com
dailystar.com.lb	realestatejuice.com
dbindex.info	realestatekey.com
dewa.com	realestaterank.com
didugetthe.info	realestateworlddirectory.com
dinosearch.com	realook.com
dir.forthnet.gr	reiclubdirectory.com
dir.megatop200.com	reidepot.com
dir.webhostinggeeks.com	reilinks.com
dir2u.com	remdirectory.com
dir6.com	resources.eu.com
directory.datenautobahn	schwoitdirectory.com

directory.inexus.pl	scoop.evansville.net
directorybin.com	scrubtheweb.com
directoryforge.com	searchit.com
directoryhint.com	searchlisting.com
directory-of-links.com	searchsight.com
directoryrating.com	searchwho.com
directoryvault.com	seekbase.com
directorywala.com	seekmatrix.com
directoryworld.net	seoweblink.com
dirnet.ovh.org	sitemapped.com
diworldonline.com	sitereviewer.net
dmegs.com	sitesdirectory.info
dmoz.org	slackalice.com
domaining.in	smallbizsearch.com
dotsterdirectory.com	small-seo-dir.com
draze.com	smartdir.info
duanegartman.com	solutionsguide.info
duune.com	somuch.com
dynn.org	splatsearch.com
easy-webdirectory.com	submission4u.com
elinkindex.com	submitlinknow.com
engravablemomemts.com	submitweblinks.com
ensurelinks.com	suggestlink.co.in
entireweb.com	suggest-link.net
erealestatedirectory.com	suggesturls.net
estateround.com	superpages.com
eVisum.com	surfcell.co.uk
ewebdir.com	surfgopher.com
ewebindex.com	swaction.com
exactseek.com	taterlinks.com
ezeindex.com	tbwd.us
ezilon.com	texas-red.com
ferretseek.com	textonlyweb.com
financialdot.com	thalesdirectory.com
findlaw.com	theclassifieds.org.uk
findlink.gr	the-free-directory.info
flesko.co.uk	thegii.com
forage.in	thelinkcatalog.com
forumurl.com	thelivinglink.net
freeadvertisingdirectory.com	thewallhut.com
freecomplex.com	top92.net
freelistingdirectory.info	topadd.info
free-top.net	topdirectory.biz
freewd.org	topdirectory.com
free-web-directory.coollog.com	toprankdir.com
freewebsitedirectory.com	toprankers.info
fsboguide.com	topsearchnet.com
fybersearch.com	totalrealestatesolutions.com
general-webiste-directory.com	trafficauction
getalink.info	turnpike.net

160

getlistedrightnow.com	ukwebmasterworld.net
gettoplisted.org	ulysseek.com
gigablast.com	urlbase.net
gimik tayo	urlclub.info
global-real-estate.com	urlmoz.com
goldenweb.it	urlslive.com
google	us-realestatedirectory.com
guidebig.com	uudir.com
	venturenetworking.com
xitepod.com	w3dot.org
yahoo.com	walhello.com
yakto.com	webdexed
yelk.net	web-directories.ws
zeezo.com	webdirectory.cn
zoomdir.com	webdirectory.net.au
123hitlinks.info	webdirectory.nu
123Khoj.com	webdirectory1.info
1abc.org	webmaster-corner.com
1kn.org	webmasterforums.net
2websearch.com	webmastertop100.info
36towns.com	webpagelibrary.com
3windex.com	websquash.com
4arabs.com	wesece.com
4-every-1.ws	wikidweb.com
4realestatedirectory.com	worldrealestatedirectory.com
777media.com	worldrealestatedirectory.net
	worldwebdirectory.co.uk
	wwws.org

HOW TO MAKE MONEY

HOW TO MAKE MONEY

GOOGLE ADSENSE

There are a couple different methods a webmaster can use to increase the revenue generated by their websites. We will begin by signing up and creating a Google AdSense ad and uploading it to our site to get a first hand look at this powerful tool.

AdSense feeds are highly customizable and typically adhere to the main theme of any website. You can set up your AD to make money from:

- CONTENT
    - Display's targeted Google Ads on your website's content pages and generates revenue from valid clicks or impressions.

- MOBILE
    - Connect your mobile (phone) users with the right ad at the right time as they seek information on the go.

- SEARCH
    - Allow your users to search your site or the web, and earn from ads on the search results pages.

- FEEDS
    - Earn revenue by displaying targeted text and image ads in your feed content, wherever it's viewed.

Let us begin by connecting and logging into Google's AdSense interface. Type in → http://www.google.com

Click on the "Advertising Programs" link as seen in image below.

Now Click on "Google AdSense". If you have not setup an account, please do so now. Once you have logged into your dashboard, it should resemble the image below:

This is your main page and allows you to see how much money you have accrued, as well as analyzing the sources from where those funds came. You will also be able to determine which of your ads are performing and which aren't. This will aid in making any needed adjustments that may be necessary.

Creating an AD

There are numerous variations that these ads can resemble, depending on the user. To simplify matters, we will choose the most generic ad format. Feel free to go back and experiment on your custom setup later.

Let's click on the "AdSense Setup" tab. Now we may create ads for any of the following formats. Let's choose the primary format and create a **AdSense for Content**.

Click on the "Ad unit" → Text and image ads (default). There are many options for the actual format or size of the ad you wish to create, seen here:

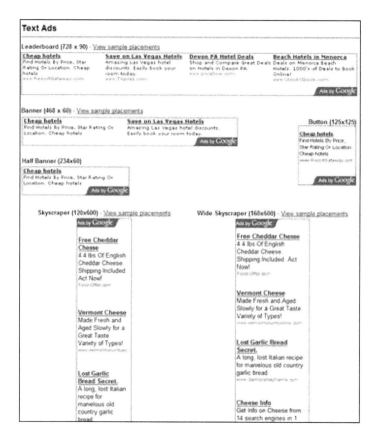

Choose your format size, color & corner styles.

More options → Alternate ads or colors (Leave Default Settings)

In the next section, you will be able to add your own custom channel in order to view the performance of different ads. You may leave this option blank.

Once you "Submit and Get Code", highlight script and paste this code into any web page or website that you wish. Location of script placement is entirely up to user.

It is important to note that it may take Google anywhere from 5-30 minutes to crawl your site to determine what theme ads to run. In this down time, it will usually run some form of Public Service Ads.

If the AdSense ads are not relevant to your website then consider increasing the frequency of your primary keywords. Use SEOCHAT.com to determine your keyword density (FREE service).

Once our website has been evaluated by Google, the REAL ads will ensue. In the example shown below, we have added the generic ad into one of our FOREX website's for teaching purposes only. As you have probably seen before on hundreds of websites, the "ADS BY GOOGLE" tag is always at the bottom right hand corner of the ads.

Any click on the advertisements by your customers, will now make you money. The ads are now set and will constantly rotate from company to company automatically.

Be very careful not to click on your own site's advertisements. Google is very adept in determining who is cheating them. You will be banned from using their services if caught.

BECOMING AN AFFILIATE

Wikipedia.com defines **Affiliate Marketing** as an Internet-based marketing practice in which a business rewards one or more affiliates for each visitor or customer brought about by the affiliate's marketing efforts.

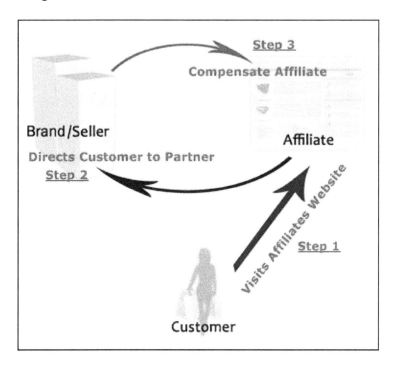

Simply stated, you get paid for selling other people's goods or services. The percentage of revenue generated depends primarily upon the Merchant.

Good Affiliate Site's

SHAREASALE.COM	LINKSHARE.COM
YOTTACASH.COM	CLICKBANK.COM
AFFILIATESCOUT.COM	CJ.COM (Commission Junction)
AFFILIATETIPS.COM	TOP-AFFILIATE.COM